Once Broken
Now Restored

Chundria De'Antae

©2017 Chundria De'Antae

All rights reserved. No parts of this publication may be reproduced, stored in a retrieval system, or transmitted in any way or by any means, electronic, mechanical, photocopying, recording or otherwise, without the prior written permission.

Cover and Interior Design by Chundria De'Antae

All scripture references are taken from the Holy Bible, King James Version. The King James Version is public domain in the United States.

This book is dedicated to my Big Momma, Lue Dell Howard. Thank you for creating an environment that allowed the opportunity for my encounter with Jesus at a young age. Thank you for loving and nurturing me those beginning years of my life. I love and appreciate you so much. You didn't have to do it, but you did it.

I also dedicate this book to my daughters, Summer and Jasiah. Everything I endure and overcome is to change the trajectory of your future. May the blessings follow you and all the generations to come.

Table of Contents

Preface
   Introduction (p.1)
Chapter 1
   The Beginning (p.3)
Chapter 2
   Tumbleweed (p.16)
Chapter 3
   Trapped (p.23)
Chapter 4
   Moving On (p.27)
Chapter 5
   Torment (p.34)
Chapter 6
   Healing and Deliverance (p.44)
Chapter 7
   Single Parent (p.49)
Chapter 8
   No More! (p.60)
Chapter 9
   The Church (p.71)
Chapter 10
   Generational Attacks (p.82)
Chapter 11
   God's Presence Matters (p.85)
Chapter 12
   Transitions (p.91)
Chapter 13
   Potter and the Clay (p.97)

Chapter 14
　　Why Jesus? (p.100)
Chapter 15
　　Unshakable, Unbreakable (p.107)
Acknowledgment
　　Thank You (p.115)
Invitation
　　Love Letter (p.117)

Preface

This book has been on the backburner for a while. It was stashed away with many of my unfinished works. I kept telling myself I'd get to it. I've worked on it a few times over the years when I was feeling inspired, but that never lasted long. Life kept throwing all it had at me and I was more focused on just surviving my day to day. Completing a book was not at the top of my list of priorities. It was mentally exhausting just thinking about the time and effort I would have to invest. Fortunately, procrastination has an expiration date. A time comes when you can no longer remain stagnate. You must move forward or fall back. That day came and going backwards has never been an option for me.

I was twenty-one when God began speaking to me about this book. One day while I was sitting in lecture, at Washington State University, I heard a soft voice say, "Begin writing your book now." Never in a million years would I have put me and writing books in the same sentence. I thought about it for a minute and then dismissed the thought. What was I supposed to write about? And who would even care about what I would have to say? A few weeks later, during a home bible study, one of the young men in the meeting said he had a word for me. He prophesied that I would write books. I instantly remembered the voice I heard in class that day. Again, the idea of me writing not only a book, but books was quickly dismissed.

On April 28, 1999, Wednesday morning, while in the shower it happened again. As I stood under the warm water singing a song of worship to the Lord that's when I heard, "*My Walk with God*". I guess in this instance third time was a charm. I knew I was destined to write this book and the story I was to tell would be my own. I began writing that day. I thought I would finish in no time. I never thought it would take me years on top of years to complete. I've been beyond frustrated at times while writing this book. It just didn't come together as quickly as I thought it would. Over the years, God has taught me the importance of **process** and **timing.** I had to live out a few more things before I could write out this part of my journey. It was experience time. Before me were years of testing for the testimony.

Now, at 41, I have completed this book God assigned to me so many years ago. This book will take you on my journey of overcoming adversity and religious pitfalls while organically developing an intimate relationship with God through Christ Jesus. Welcome into my life! I hope that as you read my experiences and the wisdom gained along the way; keys will be released in your life to unlock doors to set you free. May all who read this book be blessed.

The Beginning

"Now I lay me down to sleep. I pray the Lord my soul to keep. If I should die before I wake. I pray the Lord my soul to take. Amen."

As I look back, to think this is where it all began. This simple prayer set me on a path of coming into relationship with God. Without fail, I said this prayer every night as a young child. Never devalue consistent acts of faith. We all must start somewhere. What matters most is that we start. As I read my Bible and matured in the faith my prayers would change. You'll see how much later. Right now, let's start at the beginning.

"In the beginning was the Word, and the Word was with God, and the Word was God. The same was in the beginning with God. All things were made by Him; and without him was not any thing made that was made." John 1:1-3 (KJV)

In my beginning, there was myself, my damaged teenage mother, and a young father who was quickly settling into the identity the culture in our community had already assigned him before he was born. Though I was brought into the world through the union of my biological mother and father, I know I was created with purpose by my Heavenly Father. My parents were merely my point of entrance into the earth.

I would spend the first five years of my life living in the projects of Minden, Louisiana. It was a very small town with little to no opportunity for a poor little black girl. Even at a young age I had no aspiration to perpetuate stereotypes and become a statistic. Uneducated teenage mothers on welfare was the norm. It was a norm I wasn't willing to accept for myself. I was surrounded by poverty, violence, alcoholism, drug addiction, racial injustice, criminals and death. I was dealt a bad hand. A hand that gave me slim to no chance of winning. Unfortunately, we live in a society that has an unrealistic expectation for us all to be successful regardless of our circumstances. I had to take the hand I was dealt and make it work, but I couldn't work it alone.

"And we know that all things work together for good to them that love God, to them who are the called according to his purpose." Romans 8:28 (KJV)

As a child, I was very observant. I was a little too aware of my surroundings at times. However, I do believe that worked out for my good. It caused me to fix my mind on some things at a very young age. I loved the people, but I hated the culture of the community in which I lived. I vowed to myself my life would be different. I started off in the projects, but I was determined not to spend my life there.

I have few memories of my father at that time. As an adult, I've had the opportunity to have several conversations with him. He said he tried to be more involved, but my mother made it difficult. This I don't doubt, but it's not an excuse to abandon your child. I could sense the guilt he carried. I extended grace and exercised my patience giving him every opportunity to be honest with not only me, but himself. He later admitted that he could have done more to secure his presence in my life.

The relationship with my mother has been quite the experience. I love my mother and father. In being transparent about the occurrences in my life, know that it is not my intention to dishonor my parents. I am only sharing my story in hopes to encourage, inspire and motivate others to rise above their unfavorable circumstances. I want others to know they can succeed no matter what obstacles they face.

With that being said, I don't remember much of my mother in the earlier years of my life either. I have no memory of a hug or a kiss. I can't remember her telling me she loved me. I can't remember anything. I won't claim these things never happened, but whatever she did or did not do was not enough to leave an impression. I never bonded with my mother or father, and that has greatly affected my take on relationships. A child cannot understand all the complexities of life. My parents were not as present in my life as I needed them to be. Throughout my childhood I would struggle with feeling abandoned and unwanted. Always questioning why my parents did not love me.

"When my father and my mother forsake me, then the Lord will take me up." Psalm 27:10 (KJV)

My mother joined the military when I was around the age of three. I was left behind and cared for by Big Momma. Big Momma is my grandmother. She is my mother's mom. In my 30's, my mother told me she joined the military to give us a better life. She said it was hard to leave me behind. As a mother, I don't doubt that was the original plan. I don't doubt that it had to be one of the hardest decisions she's had to make. She probably intended to make her way home as soon as possible. As the old proverb goes; the road to hell is paved with good intentions. Her return didn't come soon enough. While my mother was away making her way in the world, my grandmother was filling the void left by my mother.

Big Momma was a character. She is the only person I've known who would praise the Lord and call someone a sorry bastard in the same sentence. She had six children, but she would tell me I was her seventh baby. She always made me feel so special. Some of my first and for a long time only memories of being loved and accepted are with her.

Every morning I woke up to gospel music. She would be in the kitchen preparing breakfast. There is nothing like waking up to the smell of sausage, eggs, grits and cheese toast. Some mornings I was treated with a cup of instant coffee loaded with sugar. Sending a small child to school high on caffeine and sugar is probably not the best idea, but these were special moments that I treasure. There would also be a hot meal waiting when I returned home from school. Most days it was a big pot of collard greens or cabbage served with some hot water cornbread and slices of raw onion or tomato. After pouring on a little hot sauce and vinegar, we'd mush it all together with our fingers. We ate with our hands a lot. If the food was too hot it would burn your fingers.

The house was loaded with religious paraphernalia. You literally couldn't escape Jesus. Big Momma had a picture of Jesus that hung in her bedroom over the center of the bed. That picture freaked me out. The eyes gave the illusion of them following you as you moved, and they glowed in the dark. I laugh about it today, but I was horrified as a child. I would tuck myself under the quilt, close my eyes tight and try to fall asleep as quickly as possible.

She had this huge table bible with illustrations. It sat on a stand all by itself. She couldn't read, but still understood how valuable the Word of God was and honored it as best she could. She made sure the Word had a place to dwell in her home. If I recall correctly it was opened to Psalm 23. The Lord is my Shepard. It was a beautiful bible. It was so hard for me to walk by without at least sliding my hands across the pages. It was the size of an unabridged dictionary. It was white leather hardback with metallic gold lettering. There were pastel colored illustrations on select pages. She didn't like anybody touching it. Before I could read, I would sneak and flip through the pages and look at the pictures. In the subtlest of ways God was drawing me to His Word even back then. How fortunate I am to serve a God who's able to communicate with us in ways beyond our recognition, so that we could get a touch from Him. He is not bound by language barriers or literacy. I would eventually learn to read and be able to explore His word, but He initiated a relationship with me years before that day would come.

That day will more than likely not come for my grandmother. It breaks my heart that she has never learned to read. She hasn't experienced opening the bible and reading a single verse for herself. The woman that introduced me to the faith will never on this earth be able to experience the Word of God as I have. Though she has a heart for God, I do believe her inability to seek His truths in the scripture and study the verses has kept her stagnate in a childlike faith. It has kept her from developing an intimate relationship with Him. I know she is saved. I believe in my heart, with confirmation in my spirit, when we have both lived out our time here on earth we will meet again in heaven. She may not experience all the benefits that became accessible at salvation during this life, but I thank God for His mercy and grace. I have peace in knowing that she has accepted Jesus as her Lord and Savior. When she surrendered her life to Him, she secured her place in eternity with the Lord. All our walks on this side of glory are unique to the individual. He is a just God that does not compare us to one another, but we will be judged on our individual walks. As believers we are living for the prize that awaits on the other side of this life.

"Better is the poor that walketh in his uprightness, than he that is perverse in his ways, though he be rich."
                                                                    Proverbs 28:6 (KJV)

She gave up the big room on hot summer nights, so I could sleep comfortably. We lived in government housing. The rooms really weren't that big, but it was the bigger room with a window air conditioning unit. She was very selfless. As I am writing this, I am realizing how much of an influence she's had on the way I parent my children. I can't believe after all these years I'm just now making the connection. I have so many great memories. I love her dearly and thank her so much for filling in that gap as do so many other grandparents.

My mother returned for me after my first year of school. I was about to be taken away from my grandmother who I had come to know as my mother. I would be leaving my entire family behind. My family was extremely dysfunctional. I wasn't growing up in the best environment, but it's all I had ever known. I would be taken away by my mother who was a stranger to me. I remember feeling uneasy in her presence. I did not want to go, but no one seemed to care about what I wanted. That's one of the things I hated most about being a child. You have no control over what happens to you. You are completely dependent on others to choose what's best for you. You really suffer as a child when those who are responsible for you are good at making bad choices.

My mother and I left Louisiana and headed to Germany. This was my first time on a plane and leaving the country. Outside of television, I had very limited exposure to the world beyond my neighborhood. When we arrived in Germany all I can remember doing was taking it all in. I was in a whole new world. I was experiencing new people speaking a new language in a new country. I was in awe. The scenery was so different from anything I had ever seen. I had accepted the reality that this was my new life. I was open to the change and beginning to get excited about what was to come.

I thought I had left all relatives behind in Louisiana, but to my surprise my aunt, her husband and my cousin lived within walking distance. Who would have guessed a little country girl would fly halfway across the world and find familiar faces? I loved the time I was able to spend with them. That was probably my first and only experience of feeling what it was like to be a part of a complete family. There was something comforting about the loving healthy mother and father dynamic in the household. Every child should be able to experience this, but many won't. I would have to cherish and hold on to these moments.

My mother was very young, beautiful and enjoying life. She had a new career, steady income, new friends and was having experiences she probably would have never imagined. I don't remember a time when my mother was not in a relationship or two. One night my mother took me along on a rendezvous to meet a man she was seeing on the side. One of the great things about being an intuitive child is people can't get over on you. You're quick to pick up on what's happening around you. One of the worst things about being an intuitive child is that nothing gets past you. A child with too much information does not always lead to the best scenario.

This night the gentleman greeted me with a teddy bear. As he handed me the bear, I asked if he was giving it to me so I wouldn't tell. You should have seen the look my mother gave me as she angrily told me to sit down and be quiet. I can see how this caught her off guard. My insight on life would always make her so mad. I was a different type of child, and I know it was challenging for her to relate to me. Me being wise for my years and my mother lacking in maturity for hers made for a very rocky mother-daughter relationship. The truth will set you free, but it will also get you in a lot of trouble as a child when your parent can't handle the truth. My mother chose to view me as disrespectful rather than face her truth. If she had spent more time focused on being a mother, I believe she would have been better equipped and more prepared as a parent. I was never at the top of her list of priorities. She just wasn't ready to slow down and be a mother. Even more, I think she wasn't ready to slow down because she'd have to confront her past and deal with her demons.

One of the men she was dating would frequently stay over. She trusted him with me. I do believe she thought I'd be safe with him. When she was away for work, I would be left under his care. Those were some of the worst days of my life. I suppressed most of these memories for years. They resurfaced later in life. He did all kinds of mean and sick things to me. This caused me to feel dirty and ashamed my entire childhood into my early adult years. I was made to stand naked in front of him in different positions as punishment. He made me bathe in hot water while I cried. When I would have to go the restroom, he would make me stand in front of the toilet with my clothes off. I was not allowed to sit on the toilet until he said so. He would make me stand there until I eliminated on myself then tell me how disgusting I was. I would then have to clean up my mess with my bare hands.

He did many other sick things that aren't worth revisiting at this point in my life. If he left a mark, he would feed me a lie to tell. By design, even if I'm afraid it is hard for me to lie. One day, he punched me in my leg and told me to tell my mother I ran into a pole while playing outside. As soon as my mother came home, I ran to her and told her what had really happened. She didn't say a thing. She just walked past me and proceeded with her evening. I don't know if she ever addressed the issue with him. What I do know is that she stayed with him. She eventually left him after he got physical with her, but I would be long gone emotionally at that point.

This sent me into a downward spiral. My days were ruled by anger and fear. I hated my mother for not believing me. Not only did she not protect me, but she chose this man over her child. Now I was stuck living under the same roof with my abuser. An abuser that knew my mother would not believe me if I told. Each day I looked forward to getting out of the house and going to school. As the school day came to an end, I was inundated with anxiety. I dreaded going home. I was terrified of what was to come. I had nightmares all the time. I would wake up in cold sweats. I would see things in the dark. My mother never comforted me. She would just yell at me and tell me to go back to my room. I would run back to my room, jump into bed and pull my Raggedy Ann and Andy blanket over my head. I would hide under that blanket for the rest of the night. It's hard to believe I didn't die from overheating. My mom liked to crank the heat up so high. I would get so hot and sweaty. I can remember it being difficult to breathe, but I was so afraid I would just suffer through the heat until I fell asleep.

My great escape was fantasy. Daydreams were my safe place. There I had complete control over everything that happened. The opposite of what was happening in my reality. I was never present in the moment. *Why am I here?* I would ask myself this question daily. I was beginning to think that maybe I was born to suffer. I carried a lot of shame. I emotionally shutdown and became very withdrawn.

I would do my best to avoid my abuser. I watched my mother love a man that was so cruel to me. This hurt me to the core. I desperately needed out of this situation. One day, while home alone I called my Big Momma and told her everything. Having the courage and intellect to pick up the phone and make that international call may have saved me. After that conversation she had a talk with my mother. I don't know what she said, but I was put on a plane and flown back to Louisiana. I was back at the place I called home, but I was not the same little girl.

It breaks my heart that it all went this way. I had not seen my mother in years. The initial months following our reunion should have been devoted to reconnecting and bonding, but things took a turn for the worst. I was broken at every level of my being. By the age of six I was already living my life at a disadvantage. There are so many children that share these experiences. Based on the communities and circumstances alone in which they are born they have been set up to fail. Everything children should be protected from; they are not. And due to their deficiencies and the adversities they face daily, moving through life becomes very challenging. Most of them will crack under the pressure because they are not equipped nor prepared to survive let alone thrive. No matter how hard they try they continue to fall short. Eventually, they will give up and accept a life less than they deserve. This has resulted in communities filled with adults and children filled with rage.

When that rage is unharnessed it will be a danger to all of society.

"If my people, which are called by my name, shall humble themselves, and pray, and seek my face, and turn from their wicked ways; then will I hear from heaven, and will forgive their sin, and will heal their land." 2 Chronicles 7:14 (KJV)

Then you have the wild cards like me. Those that are the exception to the rules. They won't settle for anything. They are driven by a voice from within. They have an ability to see beyond their circumstance and chase after vision. Even as a child I knew there had to be more to life and I was going to tap into the more. There was no blueprint given to me on how to build a better life. There was no one who had gone before me and left a path for me to follow. I would just have to chase the vision the best I could and figure things out along the way.

"Where there is no vision, the people perish..."
Proverbs 29:18 (KJV)

Never start a journey without a vision. The vision will be a producer of hope when the journey gets tough. And trust that there will be times when life feels unbearable. In those times you must remind yourself of the vision. It will be your source of hope. The hope generated by vision has encouraged and sustained me in times when I felt as if I could go no further. Vision has brought me back into focus when I've gone off track. Vision will keep you on the straight and narrow path which leads you to victory.

"Trust in the Lord with all thine heart; and lean not unto thine own understanding. In all thy ways acknowledge Him, And He shall direct thy paths." Proverbs 3:5-6 (KJV)

Through all of this, not a day went by that I did not spend time in prayer. I was never angry at God. He was my only friend. I couldn't make sense of why He was allowing these things to happen, but in my heart I knew He was for me. None of this is what He had planned for my life. I was living in darkness, but I refused to believe this was it. I knew there was so much more in store for me. God had shown me a glimpse of my distant future as a young child and that kept me hopeful. I knew what awaited me on my path and I decided to survive so I would see it come to pass.

"For I know the thoughts that I think toward you, saith the Lord, thoughts of peace, and not of evil, to give you an expected end." Jeremiah 29:11 (KJV)

Tumbleweed

I went back and forth between my mother and grandmother. Just as I would settle in to a new place, it would be time to pack my bags and move again. I strongly guarded my heart. I didn't allow myself to get attached to anyone. It made it easier to say goodbye. At this point I no longer considered any place home. The last stay with my grandmother was my 5th grade school year. My mother, her new boyfriend and I went on a road trip from Maryland to Louisiana. I remember there was so much tension in the air when we arrived at Big Momma's. My mother, grandmother and aunt were having an intense conversation. I couldn't hear what they were saying. I gauged the intensity of their conversation by their pacing and facial expressions. I have no idea what they were talking about, but it must have been serious.

Shortly after we arrived, my mother and her boyfriend got in his car and drove away. At some point it clicked for me that I was being left again. I can't even recall her saying goodbye. I later came to find out that they got married and started their new life without me. Once again, I was back in the south living in the projects. My mother and father were not present in my life. I felt abandoned and unwanted. Still asking myself why my parents didn't love me. I would get picked on in the projects for being too smart and proper. I would be teased at school for living in the projects. My teachers overlooked me in class. It didn't matter that I was a very intelligent little girl. It didn't matter that I was gifted beyond my own understanding. Most often people can't see the real you. You won't be given an opportunity to shine because of your physical appearance and the location in which you live. I felt as if I were invisible at times; a throwaway kid.

"Behold, what manner of love the Father hath bestowed upon us, that we should be called the sons of God: therefore the world knoweth us not, because it knew him not."
1 John 3:1 (KJV)

My relatives loved and cared for me the best they could, but I always felt like a burden. I also never felt like I belonged. I've always felt different, and I believe they felt it too. It is hard feeling like a stranger amongst family. And it's not that I didn't have some close relationships, but my mindset and approach to life was very different. I appreciate the roles they played in my life. Although the time with them was limited, I value it. I love every one of my relatives with all my heart. In some way each of them played a significant role in the early stage of my forming. There were some rough patches along the way, but God used the rough and cherished moments all for my good. Even if I could I would not change a thing.

I fought a lot as a youngster. I guess that's to be expected if you take into consideration the environment. I was never afraid of confrontation, but I did my best to avoid it. I hated arguing and fighting, but I was so good at it. I don't say that because I'm proud of it because I'm not. All my suppressed anger came out during fights. The uncontrollable rage was frightening. It was as if I had the strength of ten men. I'd do my best to walk away, but no matter how hard you try it is nearly impossible to escape physical confrontation in a community of people who have been conditioned to resolve issues with violence. There was no place for the weak, so you got tough fast. I don't remember my father teaching me much, but he taught me how to defend myself if I were ever attacked.

I had lots of freedom at Big Momma's. I loved going on long walks alone. They were so peaceful. I can remember the warmth from the sun shining down on my skin. As I looked up at the clear blue sky, I would imagine myself hopping along on the fluffy white clouds. I would hear the rustling of the leaves as the gentle breeze blew through the trees. I skipped along the concrete being careful not to step on the cracks. Sometimes I would treat myself when I came across a blackberry bush.

If I wasn't on a walk, I was probably sitting in the grass somewhere enjoying the stillness. I heard God call me by name for the first time sitting outside in the grass. I didn't know it was Him. Each time I would run into the house to see if my grandmother had yelled for me, but she hadn't. This would happen often. My grandmother would say to me, "Girl, that's the devil callin' ya!" I don't know why she would say such a thing. That put fear in my heart, so I ignored that voice for a time. She was obviously unfamiliar with Samuel being called by the Lord as a child. If so, maybe she would have spoken into my life differently at that time.

My cousins were my first friends. I also had an uncle that was a few years older. Several of my relatives lived in the same projects, including both of my grandmothers. Generational poverty was a family affair. My time was limited with my grandmother on my father's side. I believe that was my mother's way of punishing them, but it also punished me. My mother was away advancing in her career, traveling the world and living her life. I was in Louisiana establishing relationships with my family.

My mother detested my father and his family. She only spoke negatively of them. I loved my family so of course that was very hurtful for me. When she was angry and disappointed with me, she always made sure to stress that I was just like them. I believe every time my mother looked at me, she saw my father. And I spent my entire childhood paying the price for the pain he caused her. It is sad that she couldn't push past her pain to love me. I would ask every night in prayer for God to give me discernment, wisdom and understanding. I'm not even sure if I really understood what I was asking. I just instinctively prayed for those specific things. As cursed words were spoken over me, I would think positive affirmations in hopes of cancelling out the negative before it took root. Unfortunately, some of it stuck and would affect how I thought about myself and the choices I would make well into my adulthood.

After my 5th grade school year, I was put on a plane and sent back overseas to live with my mother and her new husband. My anxiety levels were high due to my previous experience overseas. I did not want to live with the two of them. I was fearful of what life would be with my mother and new stepfather. I didn't want to go but had no choice. Once again, I would be leaving the only family I had ever known. I left feeling alone, brokenhearted and afraid.

After I arrived, it did not take long for all hell to break loose. I was barely over the jetlag when my mother and stepfather started fighting. They fought all the time about any and everything. There was lots of verbal and physical abuse. My mother and stepfather acted like fools when they would drink. It could get really embarrassing in social settings. My mother was an attention whore. She would do anything to draw attention to herself. When my stepfather drank his suppressed anger would surface, which resulted in him threatening to hurt himself or others.

My mother was verbally and physically abusive. She was also pregnant, and her emotions were all over the place. Instead of dealing with her issues or the individuals with whom she had the problem, she took her frustrations out on me. I became her human punching bag. I never felt like her daughter. There was so much hate in her heart towards me. When I looked into her eyes they never reflected a mother's love. Something inside of her was repulsed by the mere sight of me. I really do believe she wanted to love me, but it wouldn't let her.

My stepfather was a hardworking goal-oriented man. He was always striving to reach that next level professionally. Education was important to him because he understood that knowledge gives you access to opportunity. His ambition was his best quality. That's the one thing I can say I admired about him. He was driven by status and material things. He was very harsh at times. I honestly feel he gained some pleasure from putting fear in your heart, but I wasn't afraid of him. I've never had any tolerance for bullies, and now I was forced to live with one.

It was obvious from the beginning he didn't care for me, but I came with the package. When my mother remarried, she may have gained a husband, but I didn't gain a father. He had a hard time connecting with me, and with that I made my peace. He wasn't my biological father, so in my mind he owed me nothing. However, it did hurt that my mother would bring a man into my life that was unable to love me the way I deserved to be loved. It takes an amazing man to love a child that's not his as if they were his own. It's too bad he couldn't see that I was a damaged child. I needed someone to hear my truth, genuinely love me, be a constant in my life and nurture me back to wholeness. Instead I was treated like a soldier, which only made things worse.

    My mother eventually gave birth to a little girl. I had never seen her so happy. My little sister was her pride and joy. My mother and stepfather were in love with their beautiful baby girl. I loved my little sister, but it hurt me so much to witness her parents' world revolve around her. I was forced to sacrifice parts of my childhood to care for her. From birth she would know what it was to be loved and protected. She would know what it was to grow up with her mother and father. Since birth, I had been abandoned, neglected, abused and unwanted. Each day I sank deeper and deeper into depression. At the age of twelve I was done with life. And it's not that I wanted to die, but one more day of my life as it was seemed so unbearable for me at the time. I was willing to die to end the pain. What was the purpose of my existence? Was it just to suffer? These were questions I asked God in prayer. I would get no response, but I still trusted He was with me and for me. It was so hard to stay in faith during these moments of my life. I went in and out of having suicidal thoughts. Then the day came I was ready to end my own life. I knew I would be home alone for a while, so I'd have plenty of time to finish the process. I took a bottle of pills out of the medicine cabinet. I remember standing in the bathroom in front of the mirror staring into the eyes of my reflection. I couldn't see me. It was as if I was looking at a completely different person. I had every intention to take the entire bottle of pills and would have been long gone before my parents returned home. As I began to take the lid off the bottle I heard, "**No! This is not what I have for you!**" My body froze. When God speaks, there is no denying His voice. It shook me from the inside out. Unaware, I had been in a state of slumber and I could feel something deep within me awaken. I knew the consequences for suicide would be great. I knew deep down inside that this act would not be the end of my suffering, but the beginning. In that moment, I had to make a choice. So, I chose life over death that day.

Trapped

From the age of eleven until I set off for college, I lived mainly with my mother and stepfather. My mother would eventually be discharged from the military. My stepfather remained active and we would relocate several more times before I left their home for good. Contact with my relatives back home were almost non-existent at this point. The only constant in my life was God. The only place I found security was in my relationship with God. Prayer was my safe place. Only there did I find peace. It was my time to communicate with God. A time for us to speak and listen to one another. I began to write out what I believed at the time to be my thoughts and feelings in journals. Later I recognized how this was a part of His process in training my spirit to hear His voice and developing my spiritual discernment. The more I exercised those spiritual muscles the stronger they became. The clearer His voice became the more revelation I was able to receive.

"My sheep hear my voice, and I know them, and they follow me. And I give them eternal life; and they shall never perish, neither shall any man pluck them out of my hand."
John 10:27-28 (KJV)

The relationship with my mother and I grew more and more volatile. The worst part of my day was going home. I could feel the darkness covering me as I stepped over the threshold. There was a spiritual darkness that rested in every home we lived. When I was home I preferred to spend my time alone in my room. I did my best to avoid my mother, but it was impossible. There was nothing I could do that pleased her. She would always find something to complain about which excused her to be angry. The anger would last a split second before her eyes glossed over and she began to rage. It was terrifying to witness. It was as if my mother left her body and this uncontrollable unstoppable violent force took over. There was nothing I could do to stop it. I just had to ride the wave. I could not reason with it and fighting back only fed it. Who knew the biggest demon I'd ever face would be the monster that dwelt within my mother? I was always walking on eggs shells at home. My mother and stepfather were emotionally unstable. They both had unresolved issues going back to their childhood. I never knew when either would come for me.

When I was a freshman in high school my mother snapped and came at me with a knife one evening. I am sure she would have taken my life that night had I not fought my way out of the house. I remember grabbing her arm and pushing it away. We were banging against walls. My little sister was crying at the top of her lungs. Her little eyes filled with fear as she stood there watching. I made it out of the house with ripped clothes, scratches, and red marks all over my neck and arms knowing it would only be a matter of time before I was forced to return home to repeat the cycle.

I was once attacked and kicked out the house with no shoes. I walked to a friend's house in my socks. It was wet outside, so my socks were soaked by the time I made it there. I explained to my friend's mom what had happened. She was almost more upset than me. She told me it was okay for me to stay there, but before I could even get settled in my mother had called the police. She said that I had runaway. My friend's father was an officer, and even though he didn't want to, he had to turn me in. I was taken into the station, and later transported to a group home for boys and girls. I didn't even care. I was happy I wasn't going home. I didn't belong there. I did nothing to land me there, but I guess it was easier to believe that the problem was with the child. And it did not work in my favor that I was a black child. Statistically, I'm expected to be a bad seed.

Late that night, three boys charged into my room jumping me. I fought them with everything that I had and screamed until they eventually ran back to their room. Not one supervisor came to check on us that night. I don't know what those boys intended on doing and I didn't care. I just knew that it wasn't going down that night. This wouldn't be the last time I would have to fight my way out of an attempted rape. For years I attracted that perversion. For years I wondered what it was about me that pulled on that energy.

The verbal abuse rose to another level during my high school years. I wasn't sexually active as a teen, but my mother was always accusing me of being a whore. I knew that had nothing to do with me, and everything to do with her. She was punishing me for her behavior as a teen and young woman. When she wasn't calling me a whore, I was fat or a bitch. I heard her being called these things on a regular basis in her marriage. I knew that those things were not true, but when words are constantly spoken over you, they can take root and eventually manifest themselves.

The light at the end of the tunnel continued to fade. When I reached out for help, I was ignored or not taken seriously. My mother was great at playing the victim. She managed to convince others that I was a boy crazed unruly teen that would physically attack her and run away from home from time to time. Others were aware of the abuse, but afraid to step in. They didn't want to complicate their lives by helping me. I needed someone to be my voice. I needed someone to fight for me, but no one did. I was trapped. I am so thankful that even though this was a very lonely time in my life, I knew I wasn't alone. I had God. I am so thankful that in my weakest moments I was able to lean on Him and draw from His strength.

"My brethren, count it all joy when ye fall into divers temptation; Knowing this, that the trying of your faith worketh patience." James 1:2-3 (KJV)

Moving On

I fought hard during my teen years to believe that life would get better. I had grown accustomed to isolation. As much as I loved people, social interactions were exhausting. I preferred being alone most of the time. I've never been one to enjoy crowds. In social settings I'd be content alone in a corner with my thoughts. I could never understand how this read as an invitation, but people were drawn to me. At first meeting they would feel very comfortable sharing intimate details about their personal life and soliciting my opinion. As I spoke, I could see that the words were penetrating their hearts on a deep level. I could see the light in their eyes and feel the shift in their energy. That same light that was touching their heart and renewing their minds was transforming me. It amazes me that no matter where you are in your process, God can and will still use you. The gifts He has placed inside sit there waiting to be used at His will. If you allow Him, He will never miss an opportunity to do a work through you.

"Ye are the light of the world. A city that is set on a hill cannot be hid. Neither do men light a candle, and put it under a bushel, but on a candlestick; and it giveth light unto all that are in the house.
Let your light so shine before men, that they may see your good works, and glorify your Father which is in heaven."
Matthew 5:14-16 (KJV)

I was selective and allowed only a few friends access to all of me, but I loved and had so much compassion for people. My heart would break if I was witness to anyone suffering. I instinctively gravitated to those in need. I remember seeing a homeless person sitting on the side of the street for the first time from the window of the backseat of my mother's car. My heart felt like it had dropped into my stomach. I was brought to tears. I hid my face so my mother wouldn't see me crying. There were times I was devastated that people were hurting or in need and there was nothing I could do to help. Watching others suffer and not be able to help is painful. Being able to sense the emotions of others and feel what they are feeling as though their feelings are your own takes it to another level. I found myself locking my pain away as I assisted others through their difficult times. I didn't express it outwardly, but sometimes I would get so angry because no one ever inquired about my life. How was I able to sense their pain, but they were not tapping into mine? Now I understand we are gifted differently, and it is unreasonable and unfair to expect others to give to you what they don't have inside of them to give. It would have spared me some heartache if I was walking with this understanding in those days.

    Over the years all the things I loved that made my life almost bearable I began to lose interest in. My language became jokes. I was always making everyone laugh, but inside I was sinking deeper and deeper into depression. I had a few friends over the years I was able to talk to and they were there for me as best as they could be. I continued reading my bible and I prayed taking all my concerns to God. In His presence I was always comforted, but I didn't understand why my life was this way. I knew that He didn't like that I was suffering, but there was never an answer why

He was allowing my life to play out this way. As much as I hated my life, I refused to be angry with God because I trusted Him and He was all I had.

"Blessed is the man that endureth temptation: for when he is tried, he shall receive the crown of life, which the Lord hath promised to them that love him." James 1:12 (KJV)

I started to desire more time with my peers and began to experiment with new things in social settings. I remained sexually inactive during my high school years, but I tried marijuana for the first time and consumed alcohol on several occasions during my senior year. My choices could have been worse considering my circumstances. I thank God for His mercy and grace as I tried to figure out life. I've never allowed my mistakes to keep me away from Him. He knows that real change takes time. God will never give up on us because we fall short, but we must be quick to repent and allow him to work that thing out of us that draws us into temptation.

"Let us therefore come boldly unto the throne of grace, that we may obtain mercy, and find grace to help in time of need." Hebrews 4:16 (KJV)

My last year of high school couldn't have ended soon enough. The previous summer I had worked and saved some money for my parents to help me purchase my first car after receiving my driver's license. The car was a lemon. It was an automatic, but I used both feet while driving. One foot on the accelerator and the other over the brake. This car was so unpredictable. One rainy evening while driving on a back road the gas pedal got stuck. It was a terrifying experience. I was able to stop the car with the emergency brake. I'll never forget that night or the many other scares that car put me through. It broke down all the time, but it was mine and I loved that car. It temporarily became my home when my mom kicked me out of the house my senior year of high school. I was able to spend some nights at my friends' homes. I continued to go to school every day because I had made it too far not to graduate.

One day I was called out of class to the office. The principal who had always been fairly kind to me displayed some very cruel behavior that day. She said she had talked to my mother and my mother told her I had taken the car and runaway. She requested that I give her my keys and my military identification card, or she would call the police. I gave her the keys but refused to relinquish my id. A friend living in a different city picked me up later that evening and I stayed at her house for a few weeks. I really wanted to continue to go to school, but it was impossible to get there daily without transportation. My friend and her mother would give me a ride to school when they could, but it was out of the way. I was eventually kicked out of school and this was devastating. I was being treated like a juvenile delinquent and these adults had the authority to throw my life away. The school system showed no concern for my well-being or my future. I only had one class to complete to be eligible for graduation. After some weeks I temporarily moved in with a family near my school. I was not able to return to my home school, but the school district allowed me to attend an alternative school to complete the one class needed to receive my high school diploma. There were some things that took place in the home of that family, but I kept my mouth shut. I just needed to finish the one class and be on my way. It felt like everything was working against me, but I pushed through. I graduated from high school and had no plan beyond that point.

"What shall we then say to these things? If God be for us, who can be against us?" Romans 8:31 (KJV)

    My mother and a few other relatives reached out to me begging me to come home. I rejected the invitation at first, but eventually accepted. I was really hoping things would be different. I took a year off after high school and moved with my family to Florida. I had a job within a week or two of moving there. And it's a good thing that I did. My mother had another one of her episodes while my stepfather was away. She kicked me out of the house shortly after arriving in Florida. Once again, I had to survive some unfavorable circumstances.

    I went to work that night and after talking to one of the young ladies I worked with she took me home to stay with her and her much older boyfriend. The apartment was disgusting but it was a place to lay my head. There was only one bedroom, so I slept on the couch. She was addicted to hard drugs which made this a very interesting arrangement. One day she just disappeared. We had no idea where she went. We never saw or spoke to her again. The boyfriend allowed me to stay. I paid him a portion of the rent and gave him gas money to take me to and from work. It was a very awkward living arrangement, but what other option did I have? This is the time in my life I started the cycle of dating guys that didn't treat me the way I deserved to be treated. I became sexually active, a social drinker and marijuana smoker. I stayed away from anything stronger. I was smart enough to know some drugs you don't even take that risk.

     I landed myself in some mess this year of my life. Every time I think about the things that took place, I can't do anything but thank God for keeping me. I applied for college and I was accepted, so that helped keep me encouraged as I waited out that year. My mother asked for me to come back home right before I would be leaving for college. Like a fool I went back expecting things would be different, but they never were. I had no idea how I was going to pay for school. My mother and stepfather refused to sign for my student loans. My stepfather's exact words were, "I'm not wasting my damn money on her ass!" I didn't allow the lack of finances to discourage me. I continued to communicate with God daily. My life was a mess, but we were still walking it out together. I was working with what I had; doing the best I could. I kept my trust in God believing that somehow everything would work out for my good. I left for college with a plane ticket, a suitcase, a box and $200. I was now legally an adult and starting my journey in the world on my own.

"Therefore take no thought, saying, What shall we eat? or, What shall we drink? or, Wherewithal shall we be clothed? (For all these things do the Gentiles seek:) for your heavenly Father knoweth that ye have need of all these things.

But seek ye first the kingdom of God, and his righteousness; and all these things shall be added unto you.
Take therefore no thought for the morrow: for the morrow shall take thought for the things of itself. Sufficient unto the day is the evil thereof." Matthew 6:31-34 (KJV)

Torment

During the first two years of college I endured my worst bouts of depression. I experienced dizzy spells, fainting and sleep episodes. I would sleep through days and be completely unaware. I should have died from alcohol poisoning or lost all my brain cells from the marijuana I smoked. I could have contracted an incurable sexually transmitted disease, but God spared me. He preserved my mind and body. I had suppressed my most traumatic memories and they began to resurface. I had survived my childhood and adolescent years. Now, I stood alone facing the demons of my past. The burden was so heavy It literally felt as if I were carrying the weight of the world on my shoulders. I walked around every day dragging that baggage with me everywhere I went. Confronting the unresolved issues of my past while managing the responsibilities and socialization that came with college was tough to say the least. I could probably write a book on my college years alone. God kept me through these years. All the dumb mistakes I made didn't stop Him from showing up in my life day after day. I was living and learning. Growing through every choice I made. My life was still messy, but every day ended with me being a better version of myself. God wasted no opportunity as a teaching moment.

"But blessed are your eyes, for they see: and your ears, for they hear. For verily I say unto you, That many prophets and righteous men have desired to see those things which ye see, and have not seen them; and to hear those things which ye hear, and have not heard them." Matthew 13:16-17 (KJV)

My junior year of college I began to feel a strong pull on my life in the spirit. The spiritual and natural realms synchronized. Things were being revealed that I was having a hard time processing and had no one to turn to for counsel without them diagnosing me as insane. As I awakened from another restless night, I began to wonder if this was ever going to end. Why was this happening to me? Why was it happening now? What could I do to make it all stop? I spent my days anticipating what was to come when darkness fell. Will things be different tonight? Will this all be over? Will the visitations stop? I can't explain to you in words the toll it was taking on my mind, body and spirit being engrossed into the spiritual realm. I was overwhelmed and overstimulated by all that was coming at me. The constant awareness of the interaction between people and spirits was almost unbearable. You would think the visual would have been the worst of it all, but for me it was the never-ending dialogue. There were so many voices.

Tongues I can't even describe. I couldn't filter the sounds. I couldn't adjust the volume. I just wanted it to stop. I needed it to stop, but there was no way to shut it off. At least, there was none that I knew of at the time. I wish there would have been an experienced authority in this type of matter who could have helped guide me through this process. But there was no one for me to call on.

It's amazing to think, now truly know, that so much more is going on than meets the eye. There really is no silence in the world. Someone or something is always speaking and someone or something is always receiving. If you're not hearing from a person, then a spiritual being is whispering in your ear. I know it sounds crazy to the average person, probably even to a lot of Christians, but nevertheless it is the truth. This is everyone's reality. It was a reality I wasn't quite ready for myself, and this wasn't something completely new to me. I had been tapping in and out of the spiritual realm since I was a small child, just not to this extreme. I had dreams, visions and had been hearing and sensing God for most of my life. There have been many things revealed to me concerning my life as well as the life of others. He has even shown me things that were to take place in the world. Some things have come to pass, many are still to come. The revelation of the Word of God has kept me encouraged through the years.

Unfortunately, His Word never shows up alone. Up until this point in my life, I had also been tormented my demonic forces. For as long as I can remember the spiritual realm had been a tangible world to me, just not to this magnitude. My mission in this current state was to shut it down. One of my close friends had spent the night at my apartment a few times. I thought that might bring me some peace. I thought it would take some edge off the fear, but it didn't. It was a natural solution to a spiritual problem. I knew it wouldn't work, but still went through the motions for a few days. There was nothing her presence could do for me. Would she be able to see what I could see? Would she sleep through the entire encounter? No one could help me, but God. I was so overtaken by fear. I had lived in fear for as long as I could remember, but never had it spiked to this level.

There were points of access in my life that weren't dealt with. It wasn't due to neglect on my part. I was just never taught how to activate and use the weapons that were accessible to me at salvation. I was saved and taught about faith and the importance of faith. I was told about all the wonderful things that are a part of your inheritance when you become a member of the body of Christ, but no one ever taught me how to war and contend for those things. No one taught me about the true authority I had through Christ Jesus. I was taught by example to pray and wait. Make your request and wait for God to work it all out. I never felt okay with going to God only asking Him for things and that was the gist of it all. That is not a relationship. I would always talk to Him then sit and listen. I did my best to sense His responses. Over time it became a lot easier to hear Him more clearly.

      My favorite parts of the day were our conversations. No matter how hard times were, I could always find peace in our secret place as we communed. We were establishing a relationship. He knew me and I was learning more and more about Him each day. Because of my faith, time invested in the relationship, the prayers of those that came before me, the delayed promises He had stored up for me and my family, and most of all because He loved me; life was about to forever change. I was about to be freed from many generational curses and gain access to generational blessings. I was about to embark on a journey that surpassed all understanding. I was about to start my processing season of life that would bring me into my kingdom identity. God was about to separate me from my past, which was a web of lies holding me back. He was going to develop me in the new. It was time to walk out the purposes for which I was created. The grace was gone for my old way of living and thinking. I knew I could no longer get by that way. I knew God was with me as He had always been, but there were certain things that I had to overcome spiritually. He could not do it for me. I had to activate my faith and resist the enemy. It was years down the road that I gained complete understanding of this shifting event in my life.

"Have I not commanded thee? Be strong and of a good courage; be not afraid, neither be thou dismayed: for the Lord thy God is with thee whithersoever thou goest." Joshua 1:9 (KJV)

On this evening, as I sat home alone, I was filled with fear. Day and night had met, kissed each other and went their separate ways. I was left with the darkness wishing that the new day had already come. I did everything I could to avoid sleep, until I could stall no longer. It was time. As I laid there in my bed in the darkness, I cannot explain to you in words how terrified I was. My anxiety levels were at an all-time high, but it was time. I was ready to face my fears. As frightened as I was, I was more tired of living in fear. I had lived in fear my whole life. I couldn't live that way anymore. That night, I made up my mind to have the victory. The victory would be mine. I would not succumb to fear. I would be brave, for my Heavenly Father was with me and for me. Fear is the opposite of faith. You can't be in faith and deathly afraid at the same time. I decided that night to act like I believed all the things I had read in the Bible. I decided to act like I believed all the things God had spoken to me. So I closed my eyes and after some time drifted off to sleep.

While sleeping I remember having this urge to move, but when I attempted I could not. I was being restrained. My hands and legs were pinned down to the bed. I was trying with all my might to free myself, but it was impossible. I couldn't move any parts of my body. Then a thought came to me. I would cry out to the Lord to come save me. When I opened my mouth to release a shout there was nothing. My voice was trapped. It felt like I had a blockage in my throat. I could feel my voice, the words were formed, but it was as if a wall was there that I could not push pass. I knew there was power in the name of Jesus. At the name of Jesus the enemy must flee. If I could just say the name of Jesus, everything would be okay. I never pushed so hard to speak a word out of my mouth like I did that night. I was determined and eventually the sound was released. It was weak and airy in the beginning, but as I continued to repeat, the word came out strong and firm. I didn't feel as scared and vulnerable. I felt a shift taking place in the atmosphere.

Before I move on, I want to explain what just took place. Believe it or not this wasn't the first time this had happened to me. This had taken place several times over the course of about two weeks. At the time I thought I was being restrained by some invisible evil entity. Don't judge me. I know it sounds crazy, but it is the truth. And I want to be completely transparent right now. I had watched numerous horror movies growing up that left my head filled with so much garbage that was tainting my thinking at a crucial moment in my life. I was convinced this was the work of the enemy, but it wasn't. Many years later, as I was communing with God, we revisited this moment. What He revealed to me was jaw dropping. He said, *"That wasn't Satan holding you down. It was not your physical body being held down. It was your spiritual man being restrained by your physical body. Your spirit man knew it was time to rise up and break free. There was something coming to pass that could only be overcome by the spirit. You had made it thus far primarily off of your natural abilities. The natural would sustain you no longer. I was calling you to rise up. So that night in that moment was a battle between your spirit and your flesh. Who would dominate your earthly vessel from that moment on?"*

Wow! I was speechless. I had it all wrong. That revelation changed my life. I am so glad that my spirit man rose up and won the battle that night. If it had not, I probably wouldn't be here today to tell this story.

"Submit yourselves therefore to God. Resist the devil, and he will flee from you." James 4:7 KJV

Now let us get back to that night's events. I was in an unconscious state as the struggle went on. It felt as though it lasted forever. I literally felt as though I was fighting for my life. I remember frantically sitting up when I finally broke free. I was still screaming the name of Jesus as I panted for air with my eyes still closed. It took a moment for me to fully awaken. My eyelids gradually opened and as my vision came into focus every fiber of my being froze as I beheld what presented before me. It felt like time had stopped. Everything around me had vanished. There was only me and this creature. Face to face. Our eyes were locked. I came out of shock just enough to try to think of an escape out of this predicament. There was no escape. I could sense that the only way out was to go in.

I sat there for a couple of minutes gazing in the eyes of this being. Once I made it through the initial shock I became somewhat intrigued by this sight before me. I will do my best to describe, but it will be difficult. In the physical, we can't even begin to imagine the things to be seen in the spiritual realm. The face had no expression. I could not detect any emotion. I was looking at something that appeared to be living, but I could sense no life. Its features were alluring. I would be lying if I said it wasn't enticing. For a moment I could feel myself being drawing in. Still this day I am astonished by the thought that went into the creation of this being. It was as if all the most beautiful facial features of man and animal were taken and put into this one being, and somehow it worked. It was white, but not a vibrant white. There was a glow that surrounded it, but it was a dull glow. It was very dim, as if it were going out. I could not see the body because it was too big for me to see. It spanned beyond my vision line. I didn't notice right away, but as I examined the space around me a little more thoroughly, I realized I was enveloped by the huge wings of this creature. It was an angel. Its head was shaped like a human. The gender was undistinguishable. The face was human-like. The covering of the face was like that of a horse. There was this beautiful short white hair that lay flat and smooth all over the face. Those are the only things I can describe with certainty. I really can't put much more into words, except for the eyes. The eyes were a muted black.

The angel never once opened its mouth as it summoned me. But as I gazed into it eyes I could hear it speaking to me, "Come with me". I asked it repeatedly what it wanted from me. "Come with me", was all that was repeated. I finally, very boldly shouted, "NO!" After that, all I can remember is sitting there in the center of my bed. The angel was gone. The fear started to set in again. I didn't know what else to do besides pray. I got down on my hands and knees, closed my eyes and began to pray in the spirit. I prayed and prayed. I wasn't going to stop praying until something broke. I don't know how long I prayed. At some point I felt the fear declining. I continued to pray even after a peace came over me, and I was no longer afraid. I knew that everything was okay, but I kept praying. Then I heard, **"It is done. Rest. The angels are with you."** I got up off the floor. I got into bed. I closed my eyes and went to sleep. The angel of death had come to receive me that night. While I was on my hands and knees praying in faith, God and His army of angels were warring on my behalf. And God had the VICTORY!

I can't explain the joy and the love I feel when I think about how long God has warred on my behalf. He created me for relationship. He created me for a purpose. He gifted me for a purpose. No matter what happens in life God will never give up on the future He planned for you. His mercy and grace are limitless. His love is immeasurable and incomparable. He has kept and continues to keep me. The enemy has been allowed to move in my life, but God remains at my side using the enemy's acts to develop me and assert His power.

Healing and Deliverance

"For that which I do, I allow not: for what I would, that do I not; but what I hate, that do I. If then I do that which I would not, I consent unto the law that it is good. Now then it is no more I that do it, but sin that dwelleth in me. For I know that in me (that is, in my flesh,) dwelleth no good thing: for to will is present with me; but how to perform that which is good I find not.
For the good that I would, I do not: but the evil which I would not, that I do. Now if I do that I would not, it is no more I that do it, but the sin that dwelleth in me." Romans 7:15-20 (KJV)

      I would love to say that life improved drastically after graduating from college. I moved from Pullman, Washington to Atlanta, Georgia. I figured a fresh start in a new place was what I needed, but I needed much more than that. At the time, I felt I had matured a lot spiritually, but I was still only in the beginning stages of understanding what it truly meant and how to walk in spiritual maturity. I had to go through a process of healing and deliverance as God continued to mature me in the faith. This would take years. I had survived my past, but now it was time to heal from the mental and emotional damage that had taken place in my childhood. I also needed healing from the damage I was causing myself as an adult due to my brokenness. As I delved deeper into the things of God my fleshly desires began to fall away. I lost my desire for drugs and alcohol. I can't even remember the specific moment I was delivered. As God was working on me the desire just went away. No longer did I turn to drugs and alcohol to escape my circumstances. He was all the escape I needed. It would have been great if my life completely turned around in an instant, but that's not reality. Everything in life is attached to a process. That would include healing and deliverance. Yes, I was saved and living out my life with God, but He was still working on me. It was inevitable I would continue to make some horrible choices. In my heart I wanted to do better, but just wanting better doesn't change your life.

Within a year of graduating from college, I got pregnant, married, gave birth and separated from my husband. And it all happened in that order. Yes, the young woman who's had an intimate relationship with God most of her life was still going against her better judgement and making unwise choices years into that relationship. *Why was this happening?* I'll tell you why it was happening. I had no clue what I was doing. My mother and father were supposed to prepare me for life. They hadn't prepared me at all, and they left me damaged. So there I was as an adult all put together on the outside, but inside I was lost.

I can still remember how much anxiety I felt coming home with my first child. Things were not going too well with my husband. It was only a matter of time before our short-lived marriage would come to its end.

"What therefore God hath joined together, let not man put asunder." Mark 10:9 (KJV)

This scripture stuck in my mind while considering divorce. Honestly, I really wasn't upset about the marriage ending. It was over before it started because that's not what God had for me. He didn't put this together. My husband and I decided to get married on our own. I could have stayed in the marriage and been miserable or could take accountability for my actions and cut my losses. I had once again landed myself in a messy predicament needing God to rescue me.

      I could feel the distance between God and myself. That bothered me more than anything else. My heart breaks at the mere thought of losing Him. I have never been able to be comfortable in sin, because I can feel that separation. I can feel the life leaving my body as I drift away from His will. This is the main reason I'm quick to repent and get back into right standing with God. He never runs out of mercy and grace. He continues to forgive me and then we work towards getting me back on track. Nothing will ever hurt me more than disappointing the one who loved me before I even knew how to love myself.

"And he said unto me, My grace is sufficient for thee: for my strength is made perfect in weakness. Most gladly therefore will I rather glory in my infirmities, that the power of Christ may rest upon me."   2 Corinthians 12:9 (KJV)

      I didn't have the tools needed to maintain a healthy relationship. We tend to repeat what we know, and all I had ever known was dysfunction. This was one of the toughest decisions I had to make because I would not be walking away from the marriage alone. Things were different this time. All the years proceeding this moment, God was dealing with only me. It would no longer be that way. As He reached down this time to pull me out of the pit, I came out carrying a precious gift. That gift was my daughter.

My mind needed a total reset. I needed deliverance from self-destructive thought patterns. I wish I could have snapped my fingers, and everything would've been fine. But it doesn't happen that way. Healing and deliverance take time. That change would start on the inside and eventually work its way out. God took his time peeling away my damaged layers and piecing me back together. Because I've laid it all at His feet and surrendered my will to His, He continues to transform me.

I'm so thankful for my relationship with Him. I am so thankful for his mercy and grace throughout my journey. I sure needed every bit of it. As my spirit man was being enlightened and strengthened, I continued to make stupid choices. The sinful part of me never stopped God from walking with me. It is inevitable that you will have many slipups when transitioning from living a sinful life to a holy life. In order to do better, you must know better. What He was pouring into me I would apply to my life, and my life started to change.

God has been so patient with me. He has consistently demonstrated unconditional love. Every time I fell into a pit, He was right there waiting with a way out. *Were there consequences I had to suffer?* Oh yes! I am thankful for that suffering. It made me think twice about making certain choices again. The suffering played a major role in my growth and development. I walked away from each experience wiser. God has never taken His hand off my life. He has shown me favor and blessed me the whole way. I didn't always see the blessing at the time. As I look back over my life I am overwhelmed with joy realizing His commitment to me.

Single Parent

"I can do all things through Christ which strengtheneth me."
Philippians 4:13 (KJV)

Being a single mom has been one of the best things that could have ever happened to me. This is coming from a girl who said she would never have kids. Obviously, that was me speaking through my pain. It's a good thing that God knows us to the core. His intentions and plans for our lives never change. And he never takes His focus off the end goal. He knew just what I needed to spark that fire in me, and that was my children.

I'm always being asked, *"How do you do it?"* That's not the right question to ask. *Why do I do it?* That's the question to ask. As a parent, how do I not do it? When people see others overcome major obstacles and manage to become successful; they are more than likely going to credit that to you being an extraordinary person. I am not. I am an ordinary person determined to live life at its best no matter what comes my way. I am an ordinary mother who made a commitment to God and my children to be the mother they needed and provide them an amazing life. They have been my motivation to push through.

Surviving my childhood was blessing enough. I might have been content with that feat alone, but God had other plans for my life. He preserves you for a purpose and He won't let go until His will is accomplished in your life. Having my first child awoke the fight in me. I was still standing, but I had grown weary. Yes, life was better than it had been, but I was still struggling. I was out in the world on my own doing my best to provide for myself and my daughter.

I relocated to Columbia, Missouri, for work when my daughter was two years old. I didn't want to be here, but I made the best of it. Now I've come to love this place. It was a blessing being sent here. It's not a perfect town, but it's been a great town to raise children in as a single mother. I've been in two relationships since moving here. The first relationship was a few years after my divorce was finalized. I had never felt more comfortable with someone. Everything made sense with him. And he got along great with my daughter. I thought he was the one until I got pregnant. What do you do when the father says he wants to be with you, but he just doesn't want the baby?

I couldn't believe those words came out of his mouth. It left me emotionally conflicted. As much as I cared for him there was no way I could kill my child that was growing inside of me. He had a very controlling Nigerian mother, and he was afraid of how she would take the news. His sister was very upset that I was pregnant. She said their mom would be very disappointed and I remember her telling me she was praying for God to handle this situation. She did not want me to have the baby, so I chose not to think of what her requests were during those prayers.

The time we spent together became awkward. I think he was fine, but for me things weren't the same. Now when I looked at his face all I could think of was him wanting me to kill our child. I know he wanted to be with me, he just wasn't ready to be a father. After a few weeks, with no explanation I just stopped seeing him. I know that wasn't the right way to handle the situation, but I was still at a place in my life where I handled conflict by running away. He continued to call me begging me to call him back, but I couldn't deal with him.

Sad to say, I had a miscarriage a few months into the pregnancy. That has been one of the hardest losses for me until this day. I can still remember gasping for air as I felt the life slip from my body. That night I did call the father to let him know I was having some complications, but after everything had transpired my heart was too weak to call him back to update him on the loss of our child. It would have hurt even more if I was able to detect relief in his voice as I was mourning the loss of my child. I still had love in my heart for him, but I didn't want to see his face or hear his voice.

I sank into a deep depression after losing my baby. I felt so much guilt. I thought my child had paid the price for my sins. I returned to work with no time off. I figured the sooner I moved on with life, the sooner I'd get over my loss. I can remember struggling to maintain my composure as I dressed for work and prepared my daughter for daycare. After dropping her off that evening, I got back into my car, buckled my seatbelt and turned on the car. Before I could put the car in drive the tears began to flood my face. I tried to pull myself together, but I couldn't. I cried for forty minutes as I drove to work. I could barely see a thing, but I made it. As I entered the building, I could hear the Holy Spirit softly speak.

"If you don't take this time to mourn your loss it will hurt you more in the long run."

I obeyed the Spirit. I took a leave of absence from work and sat in my apartment crying uncontrollably for weeks. I begged for God and my child to forgive me. I wasn't eating or sleeping well. I smelled horrible most days due to my lack of showers. I did my best to hide the pain from my daughter, but I'm sure she knew I was hurting.

One afternoon, as I sobbed in the shower, out of nowhere I could feel my baby's presence over my right shoulder. I remember turning quickly to see if he was there, but I didn't see him. I could only feel him. I put my head down and absorbed everything I could in that moment. His presence comforted my soul. A peace came over me knowing he was alright. And just like that he was gone. I cried a little more, but after that day I was able to pick up the pieces and move forward with my life with my little one forever in my heart. I know one day we will meet again.

"Blessed are they that mourn: for they shall be comforted."
Matthew 5:4 (KJV)

Two years later, I started to date my youngest daughter's father. I really wasn't even looking to be in a relationship, but he pursued me. I could discern that something wasn't right about him, but I chose to ignore the many red flags and date his potential.

"But I fear, lest by any means, as the serpent beguiled Eve through his subtilty, so your minds should be corrupted from the simplicity that is in Christ." 2 Corinthians 11:3 (KJV)

We led very different lives. And since he hid most of his life, I didn't know how different in the beginning. He introduced me to a lie. I entered a relationship on a lie, but it didn't take long for the mask to come off. I thought he was ready to settle down. He discussed marriage with me shortly after we started dating. The thought of marriage scared me since the last one hadn't worked out so well. I brushed it off. There was something about him that didn't feel right. I later came to find out he frequented night clubs, was a heavy drinker, he had a bit of a temper, and was having occasional sexual encounters with a woman from his past. I found out about the other woman shortly after we learned I was pregnant. I can't explain the pain of being cheated on by a man while carrying their child. After he was exposed, I began my transition out of that relationship immediately.

    Though his actions caused me a lot of pain, I chose to forgive him quickly. I had to release that hurt and anger while I was carrying my child. It was a lonely pregnancy, but I made it through on my own. There were complications during the delivery. I was afraid I might lose the baby and my health had been deteriorating for weeks, but we both survived. I remember holding her in my arms right after she was born. I was overwhelmed with emotions as I burst into tears. It was a rough delivery and I was so happy to hold her in my arms alive, well and completely intact.

    I hadn't seen her father in months, but he did visit us once in the hospital. I had no ill feelings towards him at this point. I had taken accountability for my part of this learning experience. This was another relationship that was doomed from the beginning. We didn't have a fighting chance. It may have been for different reasons, but we weren't ready for a committed relationship. My spirit man had warned me to walk away. I should have obeyed. Instead,

I let my flesh take the lead. And the flesh did what it does best. It leads you down a path of destruction. Again, I found myself crying at God's feet as I repented of my sins. He forgave me, comforted me and pulled me out of another pit. I now had two precious gifts; my beautiful daughters. The rebound was different this time. I was different this time. God had healed my heart and filled it with His love. I was whole in Him. This was the last time I would fall in this area.

"Oh Lord my God, I cried unto thee, and thou hast healed me." Psalm 30:2 (KJV)

For many years I couldn't find my way into a healthy relationship, and I can see the role I played in this. Some say you will attract what you are, and to a certain extent that is true. I do believe that truth needs to be expounded upon. I would hate for someone to interpret that as bad things happen to me because I am a bad person. That's not always the case. One thing I can say about myself is that my heart has always been full of love for people. Even when I struggled to love myself, I still managed to extend love to others. At my core was good, but I was also broken. And that brokenness was attracting the brokenness in others. Unfortunately, you never know what is attached to their brokenness until you're in too deep. That's why healing, deliverance and restoration are imperative. It's the most amazing feeling being whole; full of joy and peace. While I moved in and out of bad relationships and God was doing a work in me; I fell in love with Him. He became all the companion I needed. Life feels complete with Him alone, and no man will ever love me as He does. I know someday, I'll have to share my heart with the man God has chosen for me. But for now, I'm enjoying every moment that I have with Him.

Single parenting has not been easy. I have faced my fair share of challenges. If it had not been for God, I would not have made it. I've learned so much about myself through raising my children. I can't believe the things I've been able to accomplish. All credit goes to Him. Overall, I've enjoyed the comforts and benefits of being a single parent. I believe the bond between a single mother and her children is different. As my children have watched my tireless dedication, I can see how they have grown a fonder appreciation of me as a parent. When I'm not tending to my children, working or maintaining the home, I can dedicate the time I would spend on my spouse with God. This time can also be used for selfcare. I never have to worry about anyone undermining my authority. Granted it's a big

responsibility making all the decisions, but what I say goes. I don't have to exhaust the time and effort coming to an agreement with my spouse. Which lessens the potential stress in my life. These are just a few of the benefits of being a single parent. It took me years to see the blessings that come with being single, but I finally arrived at that understanding. Today, I'm able to truly embrace the experience and value every moment of it.

I've spent most of my years as a single mom without a support system. I've had seasons I was lonely and overwhelmed, but I pushed through. I've refused to live in poverty and have taken advantage of every opportunity that has come my way. Sometimes I had to create those opportunities. I have fought through too much to start settling now. If my children and I fail in life, it will be because we chose not to succeed. Failure has been a choice, but never an option for me. My girls are depending on me. They have been my motivation to face what appeared to be the impossible. Knowing that I can do all things through Christ who strengthens me, has been my encouragement to push through my trials. Serving a God that specializes in turning the impossible to possibilities didn't stop the trials from coming, but it has helped ground me as I've walked through my troubled times.

    The key is going into trouble knowing that you already have the victory. You cannot waver in your faith during trials. I believe that God has all power and authority. I know that I have access to that power and authority through Christ Jesus, and it's up to me to activate it by my faith. And I know my level of faith determines the measure of power and authority I'm able to access. The enemy has no power; what he does have is great influence. And that's why his greatest battlefield is in our minds. He knows he doesn't need power. He can be just as effective if he can influence the ones with the power. He can't take away your access to the power and authority granted us through Christ Jesus, but he can persuade us to forfeit it.

    In each trial we face, God is given an opportunity to show himself anew. We get to see him work on our behalf in new ways. We get an opportunity to see where our faith lies and to exercise it. About a year after having my second daughter my health went under attack. Over a span of a few years, one thing after another kept coming at me. It was a very hard season of my life, but I knew I was being tested and I couldn't waver in my faith if I was going to make it out alive and whole.

During this time, I remember being jolted out of my sleep. I went to the bathroom as we often do when we wake up in the middle of the night. As I proceeded to the sink to wash my hands, this is what I heard in a commanding voice as I stood there looking at myself in the bathroom mirror.

"***Pray in the Spirit.***"

I didn't know what was going on, but I've learned to be obedient when I hear *that* voice. I began to pray in the Spirit. After about five minutes the intensity of the prayer began to elevate. The Spirit was taking over. I was praying louder and louder. The tone of my voice turned violent. I began to hear instructions as I prayed.

*"**Lay your hands on your belly. Lay your hands on your head. Now lay your hands on your neck. Lay your hands on your chest.**"*

At this point I was about thirty minutes into the prayer. I was praying so forcefully my stomach muscles began to tighten. Right at this moment I began to feel my insides settling. And right then I realized I was being healed. The tears began to form in my eyes, as I went into praise. In the midnight hours, in my bathroom, I had a praise and worship session all by myself.

A couple of months later I started coughing all the time. It went on for a few months. One afternoon, while in the bathroom, I began one of my coughing spells while standing in front of the mirror. As I coughed, I noticed the left side of my neck bulge out. I coughed some more to be sure I was really seeing what I thought I was seeing. Unfortunately, I was. I was a single mom, self-employed, no medical insurance, barely living paycheck to paycheck thinking to myself how's this going to work out for me. I had to put my trust in God. Everything else was out of my control at this point.

At my first doctor's appointment, she was 100% sure it was a tumor. I sat there calmly after she delivered the news. I didn't speak a word. In the spirit I was reminded of what had taken place months before in the bathroom that night. God had healed me before my diagnosis. We had already warred and won this battle. After a few minutes I heard her ask, "Are you okay?" When I looked up, I could tell she was very concerned. I told her, "I will be just fine. I have two daughters that need me. And I still have work here to finish. Dying is not an option, so what steps do we take next to get this tumor out of me?"

To make a long story short after several appointments, tests, ultrasounds and scans to confirm diagnosis it was time for the surgery. Due to how the tumor was situated in my neck there was a possibility there could be complications removing it, but they wouldn't know until they got in there. The surgery was successful. My surgeon was surprised by his finding during the surgery. He stated that the tumor was much larger than it had appeared. A portion of it was hidden behind muscle and a portion of it had grown down into my chest. That wasn't the most shocking part. He stated that it wasn't attached to anything. He was able to grab it and slide it right out. And the rate at which the tumor had grown he couldn't believe it wasn't malignant. All I could say was, "HALLEJUAH!" All glory be to God! Through these types of experiences, God has personally showed me His miracle working power. And through my experiences, others get an opportunity to witness His power. My charges were all written off as a charitable expense. I didn't pay one penny. That's how good God is. My flesh wasn't always on board during this process, but my spirit and mind were never broken. And I stood firm until the flesh came under submission.

The faith with which you go into your troubles with won't be enough to carry you through and out. You will be changed during your trials if you allow God to be God. He will take you from faith to faith. I would have never tapped into all God had hidden deep within me had it not been for the bumps and turns along the way. My messes gave Him reason to pull on all the treasures he had placed inside of me, allowing me to do the work as He guided me into destiny.

No More!

"Honor thy father and thy mother: that thy days may be long upon the land which the Lord thy God giveth thee."
Exodus 20:12 (KJV)

There had been no contact with my mother for months. I actually think it was almost a year. I know that seems like a long time, but that was not unusual for our relationship. We have at times gone for years without speaking or seeing one another. I'm not sure what led up to our last fallout, but it had been a while. Once again, I had decided to be the bigger person and let her back into my life. She still had not acknowledged my experiences or taken accountability for her hurtful actions in my past. In her mind, I believe she thought she had been a good mother and I was a disrespectful and unappreciative child. I tried to put aside our issues in order for her to establish a healthy relationship with her grandchildren. That only lasted for so long. We lived far apart, so they would have occasional phone conversations. I would rarely speak with her because I felt that was the best way to avoid conflict. That never worked. My mother is the only person I know who can make an argument out of anything.

Most times it wasn't possible to hold a rational conversation. There was no point in even considering talking things out. When the phone rang and I would see the caller i.d., my spirit would just drop to the lowest of lows. All joy would leave my body. And to think this all took place in my spirit before I picked up the phone. It got old. I had to make a choice. I couldn't live like that anymore. Do I continue to put myself through this or do I cut her out of my life again? I was always told growing up you should honor your parents or there would be hell to pay if you didn't. It didn't matter how your parents treated you, even if they abused you, you were to take it and hold your tongue while doing it. I was impregnated with this deep spirit of fear as a young child that continued to grow and take an even stronger root as I got older. I found myself taking a break from her often. I was hoping that when we picked up the relationship, she would be a changed woman. I was always working on ways to better myself, and maybe it was just wishful thinking that I thought she was too. But things always turned out the same. It was a continuous cycle.

    I received a letter in the mail from my mother. I couldn't believe the contents of the letter. I don't know why I was surprised after all that had transpired over the years. I don't have the letter today. I was tempted to repeatedly reread and analyze it. I was led by the spirit to get rid of it. The purpose of the letter was to steal my joy. In her letter, summed up, she told me I needed to get myself together. I needed to let God fix me. She stated she was praying that God would change me. She insinuated that He would punish me, and she would never speak to me again if I didn't change my ways. She wrote this was her last time reaching out to me. If I couldn't be the daughter she wanted, I would be cut out of her life. The letter was lengthy. She wrote many things. It made no sense for her to write what she wrote if her intentions were to mend our relationship.

My initial reaction was not to respond. We could go our separate ways. All she seemed to bring to my life was suffering. I was at my wits end. I was beyond tired. I prayed about, thought about and talked about the letter for a few days. Should I reply to this letter, which was more like an ultimatum? If I did reply, how should I respond? I did my best not to respond while in my emotions. Life experience has shown me things only get worse when responding in your emotions. I wanted to see this situation through God's eyes. How would He have me handle this situation? During my time in prayer He spoke to me and this is what He said.

"Stop enabling her to hurt you. You coped by shutting those out that have deeply hurt you. Some you never let back in. Others you stay away from long enough to tuck the pain away within. Just long enough to believe you are over it. You give yourself enough time to come to a place where you can forgive and are able to maintain a friendly relationship with those you let back in and have continued to leave out an important step in this process. You haven't demanded that they treat you the way you should be treated. What you've done is let people back into your life and you only allow them to get so close to you. You feel that if you never let them all the way in, you can keep them from hurting you. That has never worked. And it never will. Until a person is held accountable for the way they treat you, they will continue to hurt you. Don't let anyone back into your life unless they have acknowledged the pain they've caused and have

sincerely apologized for their actions or lack of actions with remorse and have begun to act differently towards you. Real change does take time, but effort and actions start immediately. When you have made the decision to allow someone back into your life, at that moment you need to also make the choice to let them go if they return to old patterns of behavior. Life is too short. Keep it sweet by continuously purging what has or will attempt to rob from your life.

It was clear what I needed to do. I sat down and this is the letter I wrote.

March 25, 2010

Xxxxxx,
I am writing this in hopes of accomplishing two purposes. First, to inform you that I have received and read the letter you have taken time to write. Secondly, to express where I stand at this point and how I have arrived at this place. It took me several days and conversations with a couple of my confidants to be able to respond to things that were stated in your letter without being emotional and pointing the finger back at you. What purpose would that serve? This relationship for as long as I can remember has been about someone being right and someone being wrong. I've learned in relationships there is no black and white. We can never judge a person completely by what we see and their current actions and draw an accurate conclusion about who they are and why they do what they do without truly knowing

that person. Truly getting to know someone comes through trust, communication and the desire to spend time together (time shared). These three components have never been mutual, at least not simultaneously. As you stated in your letter, there was a time when we were inseparable until you left me at the age of three. I believe that you are telling the truth and I really wish I could remember that, but I can't. Whether I remember it or not, that doesn't change the fact that it's the truth. However, the fact that I couldn't remember who you were and identify you as my mother when you returned was about to greatly affect our relationship and forever change my life. I am a mother now and I can honestly say that I love my children unconditionally. They are two very different people. I see them for who they are and the more quality time we get to spend together, the more we love each other. I can't imagine life without them now that they are here. I believe for a mother not to love her child is impossible, unless they have mental illness or a serious drug habit. You have neither of those so logically that would mean that you love me. I know that it had to be difficult to make the choice to leave and I'm sorry that you were in a place in life and circumstance where you felt that was your only option. I'm not upset with you for making the best choice that you could at the time. I am thankful that I didn't get stuck in Minden, living in the projects, being raised on welfare, surrounded by no opportunity for a better life. Thank you. I hope this brings you some peace with that decision. I feel that you have carried that around for years and hopefully you can let that burden go and I don't want to ever talk about it again because that's not an issue for me. The following things I'm about to say are not for the breakdown, but for the building up of our relationship if that's where it leads. Sometimes you have to visit your past (no matter how ugly) to understand your present, so you can move forward into your future. I will keep it brief because it does us no good to go into the details. When you returned for me, like I stated before, I didn't identify you as my mother.

You were the lady that took me away from the only home and mother (Big Momma) I knew. You might be tempted at this moment to be upset. You really need to control those emotions. I know you said you called and sent me things, but I was a baby. You can hope for a child to understand your intentions, but you can't get mad at them when they don't. According to your letter at this point you were really excited to come and get me and start our new life together. And I was afraid and confused because I was being taken away from all I had ever known. I believe if we would have had more time to reestablish our bond, I would have gained trust and been more comfortable being myself and things would have been fine. But before that process was able to be worked through, I was abused by your boyfriend. I won't put his name in this letter because you know exactly which one I'm talking about. You don't need to know all the details of the abuse. I've already spent many years sorting things out with God, friends and plenty of counsel. I've made it through and I am stronger and wiser than I would have ever been without those experiences. What you do need to know is that my spirit was broken. I was afraid, ashamed and very alone. Some of the more disgusting things I wasn't able to share until I was an adult and working myself through the emotional damage. I do remember one day I was at the house with him and he left a big bruise on my skinny little thigh and *he told me when you came home to tell you I ran into a pole. I remember you coming through the front door, I ran over to you and said ***** hit me in my leg. I don't know if you did or said something to him later, all I know is that you stayed with him. And things got worse for me. There was no way I was going to risk telling you all the other things and you did not believe me. This is the time in my life that I shut down. I was now afraid, ashamed, alone and angry. As far as I was concerned you couldn't be trusted. You didn't believe me and you didn't protect me. I never reestablished a bond with you. I never trusted you. I would come to learn a child who doesn't establish a loving, trusting relationship with their mother and father as a young child will become very self-sufficient and trust no one. I don't need to write out everything that happened from that point on because we lived it. That brokenness that was never fixed affected my entire childhood. The way I felt about myself, other people and the choices I've made. I can definitely say that the ability to emotionally shut down my feelings for a person was necessary at a point in life for survival. I've built walls so no one could get in and hurt me, but those walls also keep people out who want to love me now. Every day is a challenge. I am very cautious about who I let in. Trust and respect are things that have to be earned. You don't just get it. I spent the beginning of my life angry, hurt and vulnerable. Now I have control over who I choose to be in my life and what type of life I want to have. I choose a peaceful life. I've had enough drama. You have to be willing to look beyond what you think you know about me and truly get to know and accept me for me. You know that little girl that was damaged so many years ago that went through life the best way she could. When you look at me you see a child* *that was rebellious and gave you hell. From your letter I inferred that you felt God purposed this for our lives. That was not God's purpose for my life or yours. God does not put together families to tear them apart. But he also doesn't expect us to maintain unhealthy relationships. I hope that some of the things said in this letter will help you understand my journey this far and begin to see me in a new light. Hopefully, knowing these things will better your communications with me. That little girl you said existed a long time ago, up until age three. I don't know her. She died a long time ago. I can't be the little girl you once had and view you through the eyes of that little girl. We can't go back and start over and create that bond. What I can do is open myself up to you and begin to build a relationship with you now. Allow you to know me for the first time. It won't be easy, but if you are willing to meet me there all things are possible. You are more than welcome to call or visit your grandchildren whenever you want. I've never denied you of that, but I can see how you could come to that assumption with you and I not being on the best of terms. Hopefully, you are not left offended because I did my best to write this from my point of view without blame. I forgave you years ago for all the ways in which I was wronged. I wouldn't be where I am today had I not forgiven you. A lot of people believe that you forgive and all is done, but that's not the case. When you forgive you release yourself from the burden of pain and anger caused by someone or oneself, but it is the beginning of your healing. Some healings can take a lifetime depending on what you've been through. I hope you can truly find it in your heart to forgive because there was an angry undertone in your letter. For any pain(intentional or unintentional) I am* *sorry. This is the last time I will apologize for the past, so hopefully you can accept that. I do have some conditions that I need you to commit to if you choose to develop a relationship with me. I need you to acknowledge that this isn't all on me and you played a significant role throughout the years in the breakdown of this relationship. And most of all moving forward I need you to be able to admit when you're wrong and know that everything is not about what ****** wants and feels. I'm not asking anything that I'm not willing to invest in the relationship. If you feel like you are unable to commit to a relationship under these conditions then it is best that we have no further communications. Either way it goes I will have peace. I know God's preference would be reconciliation, but if that's not possible then an amicable separation would be the best thing. Hope all is well. If I don't hear from you again, I wish you the best of life. If I do I know that you are willing to meet me at a place where we can move forward.*

Chundria

    I did receive a phone call from my mother. She made herself out to be the victim in this situation. In her eyes she had been the perfect mother. It really wasn't much of a conversation. It was her yelling out all the ways I had been an awful daughter. It was almost impossible to get a word in. Not once did she mention the abuse I had suffered. She refused to acknowledge and take accountability for failing me as a mother during this part of my life. But what she did that completely crushed my heart was defend my abuser. She blamed me for their relationship not working out. She stated that they were engaged to be married, but my being hateful towards him somehow was the cause of them not moving forward with the marriage. I was literally speechless. There was nothing left to be said. I was her child and not once did she show concern for what I had been through. I honestly can't think of a time that she ever put my needs first, second or third for that matter. I checked out of the conversation at that point. She was still talking when I hung up the phone.

I wish I could say this was the last time I spoke to my mother, but it wasn't. It was a long time passed before we spoke again. She refused to face and deal with the issues of our past, so the dysfunctional relationship continued. A mother should love their child. I just thought that automatically comes with the role, but through my personal experience it's not guaranteed to work out that way. My mother treated me as though I needed to earn her love and respect. I watched her give of herself and resources to others who didn't appreciate her. She was constantly being abused and taken advantage of which left her heart in a constant state of brokenness. She worked so hard to get others to love her, and all I wanted was for her to love me.

"The Lord is nigh unto them that are of a broken heart; and saveth such as be of a contrite spirit. Many are the afflictions of the righteous: but the Lord delivereth him out of them all."
Psalm 34:18-19 (KJV)

I remained stuck in this cycle for a few more years, until I had to make a choice to move forward with my life. You can't force people to change and you can't waste your life away waiting for people to change. Today my mother and I are not speaking. I love her and truly wish her the best in life, but my focus is on being the best mother I can be to my children.

Life has a way of always surprising us. You never know what God is doing behind the scenes. You just know that He is working. I have tried several times over the years to build a relationship with my father, but he wasn't in that place. It just never worked out. I had made peace with the fact that I may never know the love of my parents. Then an unplanned visit with my father changed everything. This time was different from our other meetings. We were both ready to move forward together and committed to do whatever it would take to build a relationship.

My father and I have reconciled, and things are going well. A lot of time has been lost. Time we will never regain. I can never go back and be daddy's little girl. As I get to know him as an adult, I'm realizing how much of me is just like him. I spent my childhood feeling alone and different. There was no one like me with whom I identified. Life would have been so different if he had been there all along. I believe he would have been my best friend. I'm grateful for the time we have ahead of us. You can never make up for lost times, but I plan on making the most of whatever time we have left.

The Church

Until now I had spent most of my life unchurched. My grandmother exposed me to the church in my earlier years. That small window of time allowed God to move in my life in a mighty way. He reeled me in at a young age. Not too long after all hell would break loose. Being that He is God he knew what was to come. I can say with all certainty I never would have made it unaware of His presence in my life. After leaving my grandmother, I rarely saw the inside of a church. My mother and stepfather weren't frequent church goers. I attended church somewhat regularly my last two years of college. This was the beginning to my struggle navigating within church culture.

I had become content in my relationship with God outside of the church. That's where I had spent most of my time in relationship with Him. From the beginning of my journey it has always been about the relationship with Him. It was all I had known. That started to change in my late 20's. I could feel myself being pulled to the church. I'm not referring to the building or the "church people". I was being pulled into alignment with the body of Christ. The ecclesia. I had this overwhelming desire to serve and fellowship with other believers, but that wasn't the only reason I was being drawn to the church. I had transitioned into an experience season. I was about to learn some tough, but valuable lessons that were necessary for the latter stages of my life.

There is a stigma attached to the church that I was able to look past in order to enter those doors. I had heard all kinds of stories about "the church experience" throughout my life. There are probably few who can say they have not had some reservations met with hesitation when it comes to church. You would think it would be easy to fellowship and serve with other believers that share a love of God. You would think that if an individual identifies oneself as a Christian, then they must surely have a relationship with God. Those were very dangerous assumptions to make. I was very naïve entering the church and was hurt by church leaders as well as members. I have often been treated as if I was less than, unless I offered something the leaders deemed valuable. I wish this experience was unique to me alone, but this is the experience of many. Believers are being used for their talents and resources while being denied the opportunity to exercise and develop in their spiritual gifts and share spiritual wisdom. In many churches there is an unspoken requirement that you must surrender your life to the head of the church in order to be fully embraced. It's not enough to submit to their authority. They want to be your God. They need you to honor and worship them.

    I have sat under leadership that manipulated the Word to brainwash and control their members. Leaders have abused their authority as apostles and prophets to speak lies to me in the name of Jesus. It is imperative that we develop in our spiritual discernment. It is imperative that we spend time with God, so we become familiar with His voice, character and His ways. That's the only way we will know what is and is not of Him. I've attempted to dull my shine, but due to those attempts I believe God has made me stand out even more. I've tried so hard to stay behind the scenes, but He continues to move me out front. Acting out of fear I was living as a lesser version of myself in front of those with influence. I'd learned the hard way what happens to an individual a leader deems as a threat. Time and time again, I have been put in a position to choose the church or God. And I've chosen God. Choosing God has left me walking alone many seasons of my life, but I'll continue to choose Him. Everything else means absolutely nothing without Him.

I honestly believe that having established a relationship with God outside of the church contributed greatly to me staying in the faith when my faith was challenged. I have seen so many people over the years walk away from God because they were hurt by people in the church. If I didn't have an intimate relationship with God, that could have been me. If I had not been able to discern the difference between the two, my life could have went in another direction. It breaks my heart knowing that this is happening every day.

I have suffered at the hands of the church, but I wouldn't take back any of those experiences. I've had to practice humility on levels I didn't know were possible for me. Now, I understand how and why we are commanded to love our enemies.

"But I say unto you, Love your enemies, bless them that curse you, do good to them that hate you, and pray for them which despitefully use you, and persecute you." Matthew 5:44 (KJV)

Now, I know how to identify my enemy. For the enemy is never a man, but a spirit or spirits hiding behind the man. Now, that I'm quickly able to differentiate between the two, I can fight the spirit and love the person simultaneously.

I've had to extend the same mercy and grace that God has and continues to extend to me. I have come to a place where I can quickly forgive and move forward in love. I am spiritually stronger and wiser. I've had to fight to maintain my individual identity and I've been shut out for not conforming. You don't know who you really are until you've been tested. You will never know who you are if you choose to live out who others are telling you to be. I'm thankful for the testing seasons of my life. I've been able to discover myself as God continues to work out all He's placed inside of me.

I've observed during my experiences many church leaders are not equipped to pastor maturing Christians that have an intimate relationship with God. That's because many of them don't have a relationship with God. Many of them know scripture, have fancy titles and influence; but lack relationship. They do well at drawing the people to the church. Leading souls to Christ, keeping them in the faith, and maturing Christians is impossible without spiritual wisdom and guidance from God. How can you do this without God? You can't. As a believer our main goal should be leading souls to Christ, not growing a fan club.

Every church I've entered has established its own culture. If that culture is God centered, I've had no reason for concern. God made us all unique and that should reflect in our personal lives as well as our cultures. When God is not at the core is when things go very wrong very quickly. Integrating and navigating within a church's culture while maintaining your identity, continuing to mature as a believer, and keeping God first in your life can at times present a problem.

Do I believe there are some great churches and church leaders out there? Yes, I do. I also know there are fewer than you think, and hard to come by. It took me forty years to find one, but now I am attending a church with an awesome pastor. He has a heart for God and all people. He is not afraid to preach the truth. He preaches the whole truth, not partial truth. These leaders are hard to come by. Through my personal experiences, I have come to see that churches can have everything or absolutely nothing to do with God. Outside of relationship with Him, it is guaranteed you will not always be able to tell the difference. There are many that call themselves Christians, but how many of them are true believers walking in relationship with God?

I would have never imagined how many churches and the cultures within those churches are corrupt. We should never expect any church to be perfect because people aren't perfect, and people make up the church. We should be able to expect love and respect for all people and immorality to be checked across the board. From the pulpit to the pews, all men should be held accountable for their actions. They should be corrected in love by spiritual leaders that can be trusted. I have seen many Christians turn away from God and rest their lives in the hands of men that shouldn't be trusted.

I believe having an anointed spiritual leader is very important in the lives of all believers. When I was younger, I didn't understand the value of such a relationship. Now I see how vital it is, but I've also come to see there are few such individuals out there that can be trusted with this function. I have prayed for God to connect me to authority figures that I could trust. Initially, it didn't seem like such an unreasonable request, but over time it proved to be so.

Before I go any further, let me clarify. Yes, God is more than enough. I am complete, filled and without lack in His presence alone. But He has more for us. Not only does he desire to fellowship with us, but He desires for us to fellowship with one another. He requires us to live a life where we simultaneously function in the roles of student and teacher.

"The spirit of the Lord is upon me, because he hath anointed me to preach the gospel to the poor; he hath sent me to heal the brokenhearted, to preach deliverance to the captives, and recovering the sight to the blind, to set at liberty them that are bruised." Luke 4:18(KJV)

We will always be His pupil, but He will also place men on our path to pour into us. We will also be given the responsibility to pour into others. We must be especially careful of what we deposit into those He trusts us to pour into.

We should NEVER stop checking in with God on our personal progression. When we stop checking in with God it is only a matter of time before prides sets in. We will eventually become unteachable, untrainable and unchanging. You can start with a pure heart and right intentions, but that's not enough to make it to your end destination. Maintaining a pure heart and right intentions along the journey will. You cannot do this without the continuous counsel from God, and some of that will be through authority figures that He places in our lives.

We must continuously resist the spirit of pride. Pride is a well thought out weapon for the self-destruction of mankind. When we are in pride we are literally the culprit to our own demise. We destroy ourselves. Most often we recognize it in its easily detected form; arrogance. And though all pride should be dealt with, I've found that in my life it's not the obvious pride that has been the most dangerous. It is the hidden pride. We should always go to God asking Him to reveal those hidden things to us. Whether they are good or evil, the hidden things play such a major role in our lives. They affect the way we perceive and process information. Ultimately, influencing every choice we make.

    I am so thankful for all that God has revealed to me. Layer by layer together we have tackled some hard issues that left me damaged. I'm so happy that He has been in control. He has exposed the ugly parts of me little by little. He has the best intentions for us. We can't handle the full truth about ourselves at once, but if we stick with the process we can and will be made whole.

    Unfortunately, many spiritual leaders chose to bypass the complete process of healing and restoration after deliverance. They get a little revelation, build their own platform and go straight into ministry. And that brokenness that remains will eventually show up in their ministry. When we break free from the bondage of our past, it's an exciting time. I wanted to share the good news with everyone. I wanted to share my God with everyone. I couldn't stop talking about Him and how great He is. God blows your mind with fresh revelation as you spend time with Him. You begin to share this revelation with others.

They are enlightened as well. As God feeds your spirit, He's also equipping you to feed others. In turn, they go out and speak life to those in their lives. What an awesome space to be in spiritually, but also a place to be aware of the spiritual plots and schemes being formed against you.

We must be wise and never underestimate the cleverness of the enemy. He knows when to make his move. He knows how to exhaust the least amount of effort to get maximum results. He will not come after you until you are a threat. You are not a threat until you take an active role in the body of Christ. At this point, WATCH OUT! Satan will wait until the perfect moment to infiltrate. He waits on a moment in which he would be undetected. He waits for you to get comfortable in your role. Where you once were humble and leaned on God for understanding, you now lean to your own understanding. Where you once gave God the glory, you now take the credit for His great works. That's all he needs. In an instance, a shift occurs. You are now an agent of the enemy and completely unaware. You are no longer being guided by God. The enemy has crept in, changed the agenda, and you are none the wiser.

There are many spiritual leaders standing before Christians leading them back into bondage in the name of Jesus. Instead of setting the captives free, they are being led into idolatry in the name of Jesus. I've witnessed this too many times. I have shed many tears. Tears for those who have not yet come to know God in the way I have come to know Him, so they are easily led astray. I have cried tears because my God continues to be misrepresented and accused of wrongs He has not committed. We need to stop blaming God for the things we do to ourselves. We are sometimes hurt by others, but most often we are just suffering the consequences of our sins. It is hard to see correctly in pride while living a sinful life. Without the guidance of the Holy Spirit, we will repeatedly trek down some dangerous paths.

     A great lesson I've learned in life as it pertains to the Spirit; if you are sensing that something is not right, remove yourself from that situation. There are always warning signs you are being led away from God. Don't ignore them. It never ends well for you. Trust me. If you entertain seducing spirits, they will pull you into deception every time. I know exactly what some of you are thinking right now. You're thinking you have enough sense not to fall into that trap. I have learned not to be so sure of oneself. It wouldn't be deception if we knew we were being deceived. You can be savvy in the natural, but the spiritual realm is an entirely different playing field. You need spiritual wisdom, spiritual knowledge, spiritual understanding, spiritual gifts and spiritual authority through Christ Jesus to war and win in the spiritual realm.

     God must shine His light on deception. When He does, we must trust His prompts and obey without delay. Remove yourself immediately from the place that has lured you into bondage. God will remove the veil so you can see. He will remove the blockage from your ears so you can hear. He will soften your heart so you can receive from Him. If you stop checking in with God because you feel you have it all under control it will be impossible for you to be delivered out of deception. He is the only way out.

"Trust in the Lord with all thine heart; and lean not unto thine own understanding. In all thy ways acknowledge him, and he shall direct thy paths." Proverbs 3:5-6(KJV)

What do you do when the church does not reflect God? Run! Seriously…RUN! I would argue that as a believer this is probably one of the top three hurts you will experience. When the group of individuals you turn to seeking solace abandons you; it hurts. When the group of individuals you've been working and fellowshipping with for the sole purpose of kingdom building turns its back on you; it hurts. When they not only turn their back on you, but intentionally strategically begin to rip away at your soul by starving out your spirit; It REALLY hurts!

I've watched others turn away from God as they've experienced hurt in the church. I've watched others turn away from God in church because they were led into idolatry. My response was the opposite. I grew closer to God as I experienced the pain. He comforted and counseled me. He used these as teachable moments. I had so many questions, that only He could answer. Many times His only response was to just trust Him, so that's what I did. While others were falling away, I continued to grow in faith, mature as a believer and continued getting to know God in new ways. I got to know God in bigger ways.

God, I thank you for being who you are. Without you we would be and have nothing. There is no way we could maintain a state of peace or have an unshakeable joy without you as our source. Over the past few years, I have personally witnessed unimaginable wrongs done in your name. Oh, how it must pain you, if it weighs this heavy on my heart. Father God, I ask that you continue to remove the veils so the church can see. I ask that you continue to remove the blockages from the ears so the church can hear. Father God, I ask that you continue to soften the hearts and increase the church's capacity to receive from you. How can the church set the captives free if a majority of it remains in bondage? I pray for a breakthrough in the church, so it can begin to move in new ways. I thank you in advance for the victory! It is already done! The battle is already won! Jesus fulfilled it all at the cross! In Jesus's name. Amen.

Generational Attacks

Each one of us is born with a burden to bear. This is a reality that no one can escape. We are born infected and our lives at birth are already affected by those that have come before us. Many of us inherit generational curses that can potentially determine to a great extent how we live our lives. We go through life with the best intentions, and somehow, we continue to fall into the same mess in certain areas of our life. Then we begin to look at our families and in doing so we realize that certain patterns of behavior seem to repeat themselves generation after generation. I don't know if I could even put into words how I felt when I had this epiphany. I thought I had total control of the choices I'd been making, only to realize there were other forces strongly influencing my decisions. So, in all actuality, I really wasn't in control of my life. This was a wake-up call that drew me closer to God. I needed answers that only He could give. I needed Him to shine His light on my life and expose the hidden things, and as we spent time together that is just what He did.

When we really get down to it, the only thing we control is what we allow to influence our choices. Will we be guided by God or will we let Satan lead us down a dark path towards destruction? Every choice we make is a choice between life and death. This is not to scare anyone. I'm only expressing what is true. The enemy has done a superb job at deceiving many into believing they are in total control of their lives, but they are merely puppets and he is the world's greatest puppeteer.

In general, Christians and those of the world have become a people with no accountability. We have allowed a culture to be established that has taken the weight off our responsibility for the choices we make in the natural, but that doesn't change the impact they have in the spiritual realm. That doesn't cancel out the consequences in the spiritual realm that will ultimately manifest in the natural. God is unchanging. He is the same yesterday, today and forever. He will not change His ways because we change our ways. He is God. I can't believe how many things once forbidden have become acceptable over time. As we continue to turn a blind eye, the list continues to grow by the minute. Every choice we make is a choice between life and death. We can no longer be afraid to express the truth that God has given. We live in a world in which people walk around as slaves believing they are free. There are no physical shackles or chains. They are enslaved in their minds. Their spirits are not free. I have come to see that shackles, chains and bars can't hold you captive. You can physically be restrained or confined and still be free. You can still have great joy and peace. You can still hope. You can still love and encourage. God can still plant seeds in you, water those seeds, shine His light on those seeds and produce great fruit in your life even in a dark place. We live in a society where people have been convinced that God's truth is a lie, and Satan's lies are the truth. Bondage is viewed as freedom and true freedom is considered to be bondage. We are living in an age of deception.

God give your people the eyes to see, and once enlightened, the courage to walk away from deception. Give them the holy boldness to go out and set others free with the godly wisdom you have poured into them. Let their testimonies of overcoming be used to set many others free. May it all be for your glory. In Jesus's name. Amen.

God's Presence Matters

    Race has always been a touchy subject. By touchy I mean emotional. It's taken me 40 years to tackle this topic. It takes a great amount of self-control to have a productive conversation that will move us forward in a way that would bring about unity instead of widening the gap of division. Growing up in the south you become familiar with racial divisions at a young age. I was taught to stick to your own. Don't trust whites. Especially, not white police officers. This was a necessary way of thinking in order to survive in that environment. After leaving, it was an ongoing battle resisting those thoughts. I still battle with some of those thoughts today. I could care less about the color of someone's skin. People are people and at the end of the day we all need and want the same things.
    My opinion of white police officers was formed at an early age. The relationship with the police and those in the community wasn't the best. I felt they were all bad and could not be trusted. I was taught not to trust any white person. I was taught they were all devils and should be feared. I know there are many who fault the black community for influencing their children to think in this way, but they did it and continue to do it out of love laced with fear. I was born in the late 1970's. I spent many of the earlier years of my life being raised by my grandmother. My great-grandmother was still alive with her share of stories to tell. My parents, aunts and uncles had survived the south during the Civil Rights Movement. All of them were born, raised and many still residing in the state of Louisiana. They had suffered or witnessed suffering at the hands of

whites. I may not have survived that time. If I did, I may not have made it out mentally and emotionally stable. As we were being raised their main goal was keeping us alive. We were taught based off their experiences. They were the survivors of a time that had passed, and they were left imparting into a transition generation coming up in a world that was quickly changing. It was all done out of love.

While traveling to and living in different places, I've realized we live in a world that puts whites on a pedestal. In American culture it is the standard to which we are all being held. I've been privileged to meet and befriend people from many different races and cultures. This has absolutely been one of the greatest things that could have ever happened to me. Venturing outside of my community has opened my eyes up to more than I would have ever known, but I could sense. I've come to see that the world is more than black and white. People come in so many shades and colors and we are all beautiful and uniquely gifted. There are so many wonderful cultures to be experienced.

It is not easy being a person of color in America. It's an experience that can't be explained; only lived. Imagine having to take into consideration the color of your skin when making life decisions. Imagine being prejudged and treated unfairly because of the stereotypes attached to individuals that look like you. Imagine being reminded daily that you live in a society that undermines your intelligence and your humanity. Imagine being reminded daily that you are not perceived as beautiful the way God created you. These are just a few things you are affected by as a person of color in America, that could weigh on your spirit.

I have always wanted to trace my ancestry, but it's nearly impossible tracking down any records from the past. I have so many questions about my ancestors, but my history has been lost. It's as if they never existed. They suffered through much so I could be here. The least I could do is remember and honor them, but I can't. Over the years, I have been frustrated and shed tears as my search continually led me nowhere. I may die never knowing my origins in the natural, and with that I have made peace.

I have managed through much effort to break free from a system that was not put into place for my success. All credit due to God. He showed me who I was in the spirit. From Him I came and one day will I return. That's the only identity that really matters in the end. I now live a life of which I can be proud. It affords me opportunity that others may not have, but it all came at a high price. I had to walk away from everything. I walked away from family, friends, my home and the old me. It wasn't easy, but that was the only way I would break free.

Racism can't hold me back. God won't let it hold me back. Does it make things harder? At times it does. I still experience racism on a regular basis. It shows up in many different forms, and it hurts. My heart aches for the many others that are suffering on both sides of racism. My heart aches for those it has paralyzed, but God doesn't allow the obstacle of racism or the pain it causes to be an excuse to keep me from moving forward. I don't exhaust my energy trying to get others to understand the sting of racism. I can share my experience, but I can't allow myself to be angry because someone can't personally understand it. Having the same discussion repeatedly hasn't and won't work.

Repetition doesn't always bring understanding. I've grown comfortable with the fact that I wasn't meant to influence everyone. Not everyone will relate to my experience, and that's okay.

I serve a God that loves and protects me. He continues to make a way out of no way. What comes against me doesn't change the plan He has for my life or His ability to see it through to its completion. He is God, and very aware of the world we live in. He makes no mistakes in His designs and that includes how He formed each of us. I believe every detail has its purpose. I am a black woman on purpose for a purpose. I am responsible for using these characteristics for the good of the world. With 100% confirmation in my spirit, I know that there is only one way to end racism. God is the answer. If our movements are not leading people to God, it is foolish of us to expect change. He is the only one that can transform the hearts and minds of men. The problems will remain and continue to get worse if we refuse to take our hands off the reigns and allow Him to be God in our lives on the earth. Remaining angry or dwelling in our feelings because we are being shortchanged accomplishes nothing that will contribute to the advancement of humanity. It distracts and keeps us in a stagnate state unable to move forward.

I used to feel sorry for myself. I've been hurt a lot in life. We all have. I didn't deserve most of what came my way. There was a time I believed my shortcomings were holding me back. One day, I was home thinking over my life. In that moment God must have been tired of my pitiful thinking and decided to do something about it. What He did was broaden my perspective. And He did that in a way that only He can.

In an instant, it was as if I had been transported out of my body and was taken on a journey around the world. He allowed me to peak into all the pain and suffering going on across the earth. At first, I thought I was tapping into the emotions of all those I was viewing. It was an overwhelming experience. My heart hurt on levels I didn't know were possible. Then I realized, He was allowing me to experience only a portion of the pain He feels as He looks upon the earth and watches mankind suffer. He took me on a journey that I could have never taken in the natural.

I never felt sorry for myself again after that day. I went through some terrible things, but life could have been much worse. It was time for me to grow up, and help others overcome. I would be held accountable for sitting idle while others suffered on my watch. It was my responsibility to use everything I had gained from my experiences for the good of others and it would be all for God's glory.

My grandmother was a living manifestation of faith. She was a walking miracle. For a long time, I would refer to her journey to remind me of God's miracle working power. This was a woman born in a racist south in the early 1900's. She had to drop out of school at a young age. She could not read or write. She was poor. She was black. She was shot in the back by her husband who left her to die. She wasn't supposed to live through the night, but she did. She was never supposed to walk again, but she did. Yes, she was crippled, but she could walk. Her faith carried her through all of that, and that's what I come from. I come from a line of fighters. It's in my DNA. If she was able to survive all of that, what excuse do I have for being unsuccessful in life? I continue to remind myself that racism is an obstacle, not an excuse.

Transitions

One of the most important components to living a happy life is balance. I haven't come across a man or woman living a life they truly enjoy if there is no balance. We are constantly in the act of balancing work and our personal life. We stretch ourselves thin most often between our family and friends. We struggle with meeting the needs of others and still somehow trying to have time for ourselves. We go back and forth between being responsible and disciplined to indulging in fleshly pleasures. We must learn to have a healthy balance between our natural and spiritual life. I could give many more examples, but I know you get the point.

It has not been easy to accomplish balance in life. I've really had to work at it. At times it seems impossible, but it is possible. After you finally achieve it, you'll have to work to maintain it. And no matter how much effort you put into it, it is inevitable that at some point you'll find your life out of balance again. I speak from experience. That's because we change. The world around us changes. Our circumstances change. It is a part of life to shift from one season to the next. Most often we miss that shift. We go about business as usual, but we can sense the climate has changed. What we were doing no longer get us optimal results. As a matter of fact, we may begin to see little to no results following our efforts. The shift's purpose is to push you to the next level. You won't sustain doing what you did at the previous level. You are forced to mature and walk in greater authority and contribute at a greater level than in the season before.

As I was completing this book, God was transitioning me to the next level. Everything around me completely changed. All the things I was able to count on in one season, I could no longer trust. There was a shift in my mind which changed my thoughts and my perspective. The relationships in my life took the biggest hit. It was as if God took a light and illuminated everything that had been hidden in the dark. He exposed all things that weren't of Him. He gave me the opportunity to cut those things out of my life because they could not go with me into my next season of life. And they would keep me from moving forward. He was turning my heart completely back to Him in areas I didn't realize I had drifted away.

I believe God leans a little closer to us during our times of transition. These are the crossroads of life. He loves us. He wants the best for us. He wants us to reach our full potential in life. And He goes far and beyond to help us not miss the major shifts in our lives. He speaks directly to us. He tells us the way we should go. He also strategically places people in our lives that he speaks through that confirm what He has already spoken to us. I am grateful to all those that have been bold and obedient to speak the words that God gave them for me. These confirmations encouraged, empowered and helped push me into the next level at every stage of my life.

I believe it is important to give thanks to those that have helped us along the way. It encourages the encourager to acknowledge how their actions have contributed to our progress. Throughout life we will receive from others, and God will also use us to speak into lives. Near the beginning stages of completing this book, I was going through a very tough time in the church. Many of the members were experiencing spiritual abuse from the leadership. I was very involved in the ministry and was constantly seeking God for answers. I was checking in to make sure I wasn't the problem. I was open to correction if it was needed. But if I wasn't the problem, I wanted to handle the situation in a way that wouldn't ruin my witness.

There was an event held at the church on a Saturday morning. I'll never forget the day. One of the guest speakers was this little blonde lady on fire for God. You couldn't deny her anointing. As I sat in the audience listening to her minister, she pointed to me and called me up. After I made it to the front, I can remember her gazing into my eyes. I could feel the spirit within her connecting to the spirit within me as she spoke these words over my life at such a key point for me. God was bringing me into my kingdom identity. He was preparing me for the launch into my kingdom purpose at the appointed time that He had set for me.

"Chundria. Beautiful. Beautiful woman. Beautiful woman of God. Beautiful. God made you stunning. You are stunning. God says, just as the beauty is on the outside, so is the beauty on the inside. And he says there are those who don't understand you. They don't understand the decisions you've made. They don't understand the walk you've chosen to walk. And he says, they have come against you to where you would feel sometimes you question. Would it be better? Would it be easier to not have to continue to fend off all that stuff? God says, No! He says, "Cause it's for My glory. For My glory. And He says, I am shutting their mouths. Right now! He

says, Right now I am sending warring angels on your behalf and that oppression, that distraction, that irritation is going to be gone. He says, No more! These attacks, they may have been formed, but they are not going to prosper. They are not going to come against you. They are not going to mess with you. Cause God says, I am taking you to a new place. And I see him increasing finances in your hands. I don't know if it's a promotion on your job or if He's given you a business idea to venture out. I see more in your finances coming through. And God's going to give you favor with some people that you've really wished you could kind of connect with some people. And He says, I'm going to give you favor. And I don't know. This may sound silly, but I see you modeling. I do. I just see you modeling. I don't know, but I think you look like a model. But God says, He is going to take away the accuser from the situation. This harassment is enough. He says, I'm bringing you to a place that you're going to find a new freedom in me. And He says, I'm going to allow you to understand some things that you haven't allowed in the past. It's time. It's time. You've been strong. You've been firm. You've been steady. You've been diligent. And He says, there's even been times when you said, "God, I really don't understand why I'm doing this. And it's not the easiest thing, but I want to do this. I want to do this. I want to do everything that I'm supposed to do." And God says, that gave me a big old smile. He says because I can see that tenacity rising up that I put inside of you. The thing is people think when they talk against you that they are going to cause you to breakdown, but usually it causes the opposite reaction. You say, "Ha ha. I'll show you!" And He says, you have shown them for my glory. He says, you just carry on. Me and you are going places. And I am revealing myself to you in brand new ways. He says, you get ready to start receiving those dreams. And I'm going to give you interpretations of those dreams. And I see you devouring all the information you can get on it. Then taking it to God and saying, Is this right? So, God is going to use you. Don't you give up. You've just started this journey. You've just started. Yes, ma'am. God has your back. He has taken care of it. Don't worry. Don't worry. Alright. Amen

Glenda Bradley (6/7/2014)

    She had never met me and had no idea of all that had and was transpiring in my life, but this prophetic word that went forth through her was filled with confirmations. It wasn't meant for her to understand or even you to fully understand as you read it. But for me it meant and spoke volumes. It was the word of knowledge I needed to encourage and strengthen me to push through that season of my life. I knew there were great things waiting on the other side, and God used her to remind me at a time I was beginning to grow weary.

    June 19, 2014, as I sat in the backseat of a car on my way to Lambert International Airport in Saint Louis, Missouri, I remember staring out the window looking at the corn fields. They went on and on. I remember thinking someone had planted those seeds. Someone had tended to the seeds. And from those seeds came all this corn. In that moment, this was dropped into my spirit.

It's harvest time. This is it. The time is now. Many have been called, and He has been watching over the many. Now He is plucking His few out of the many that he can send. It's sending time. The world is waiting. Now is the time for the Army of the Lord to go deeper, to rise up and go forth into the world harvesting all that are ready to be picked. It's kingdom building time.

It's not always easy as we walk with God. Sometimes you will endure long harsh seasons. You'll feel like quitting and many do. If you are reading this right now, I encourage you to keep moving. No matter how unbearable life may seem at times; push through. If you keep moving, it is guaranteed that life will get better. In my darkest moments, when there was no trace of light, and I was standing on my faith alone; God was still using me. You just might be the vessel He is intending to use to shine light into someone's life. Be encouraged.

Potter and the Clay

"But now, O Lord, thou art our father; we are the clay, and thou our potter; and we are the work of thy hand."
Isaiah 64:8(KJV)

    He is the Potter and we are the clay. He starts with a solid, heavy block of clay. It has no function, but it is pliable. He sees something great that it could be. He sees something great that we could be. He has the vision, creativity and skill set to bring that vision to life. He softens the clay with water. God softens our hearts so we may be receptive to Him. As He adds the water to soften the block of clay, He begins to spin the mass of clay. God allows our world to spin out of control. It is turned upside down. We are spun until there is almost no resistance left in us. It is a humbling process. It is what needs to take place in order to see differently.

    In the spinning our perception is changed. We begin to let go of our will and surrender to His. During the spinning process it becomes easier for the potter to manipulate the clay. Now, he can begin forming it into what he wants it to be. He continues to add water as it is needed. And it is needed throughout the process. As God forms us, it is imperative that we are continuously feeding off the living water. Throughout this process we call life, we have experiences that drain us. They leave us dry. We encounter circumstances that bring us to low places, where our hearts are hardened. The Holy Spirit and the Word sustain us in these times. Consistently consuming them allows for our heart to stay open to God and what He is doing in our lives. If our hearts are hardened towards Him, he is unable to move in our lives as He wills.

God, thank you for watering us in the dry places. Thank you for pouring on us even when we're tempted to harden our hearts toward you. Thank you for Your never-ending supply of living water that quenches our thirst. Thank you, God, for the sustenance that only You can provide. Thank you for sustaining us through the processes and processing of life. Thank you for being a God that is more than enough. In Jesus's name. Amen.

Eventually, the potter's vision begins to take form as he brings it to life through this process. It is no longer just an image in his mind, now anyone in the vicinity of the potter can see that this clay is taking on the form of something. They may not know what is being formed, but there is evidence that something is being formed. The potter started with a vision, that only he had privy to. But now others can see what they were unable to see before he began to bring his vision to life.

God will show us things at times that no one else is able to see. He gives us the vision and it is our responsibility to bring that vision to life. That is our assignment. We cannot force our vision or understanding of revelation on others. What we can do is rest that vision in God's hands. Trust that He will bring it to pass. Trust that the provision is already there. And know that in due season, He will bring along others that share that vision. They will walk alongside you and together you will bring that vision to fruition.

God, thank you for fresh revelation, fresh insight and vision that You have given to each man. Even when others cannot see or comprehend what we have been given. May we be bold and strive always to finish the work you've given us. In Jesus's name. Amen.

Now through the watering, spinning, stretching and pulling a pot has been formed. The pot starts off small. The potter can stop here, but he continues to water, spin, stretch and form the pot until it has reached the desired size. What started out as a vision has now been shaped and formed and is now ready to be filled to its capacity.

Thank you, God, for life processes. Thank you, God, that when we appear to be nobody in the natural; you see beyond the natural. You see what we could be. You see who we were created to be, and then begin a work in us. And you won't stop until you finish. Thank you, God, for taking us from faith to faith. From glory to glory. Thank you for the constant stretching. Thank you for increasing our capacity to receive through the stretching, so that we can receive the fullness of what you have for us. Thank you, God, for being the Potter that saw the potential in this clay. In Jesus's name. Amen.

Why Jesus?

"For God so loved the world, that he gave his only begotten Son, that whosoever believeth in him should not perish, but have everlasting life." John 3:16 (KJV)

Jesus is the way, the truth and the life. He is the only way. Many of our introduction to the faith are teachings about Jesus. *Jesus Loves Me* was probably one of the first songs you learned in church as a child. In Christianity we are taught that it is all about Jesus. Because He came, died and conquered the grave we have been redeemed and are no longer in bondage to sin. If we accept Him as our Lord and Savior. The Word teaches us that through Jesus alone are we saved and grafted into the body of Christ. This is all true, but I'm afraid this is where most Christians get stuck in their walk. This saddens me because there is so much that waits on the other side of salvation that most Christians are not tapping into. You must go deeper in order to access all that Christ's sacrifice made available to us. Jesus's sacrifice wasn't so we could only be saved. And though we are expected to bear witness and lead others to Christ, His sacrifice was for far more than that as well. It was to serve a much greater purpose. And because many Christians will never go deeper then foundational teachings, they will never attain what's waiting for them on the other side of salvation. All because they never stop to ask one simple question. *Why Jesus?*

One of the great things about God calling you as a child is that you ask a lot of questions. You ask questions because you are genuinely seeking understanding. Until things register in your heart and mind you will continue to ask questions. Even if that means asking the same questions many times until the answers are communicated to you in terms you understand. Sometimes the answers don't change, but as you develop and mature you begin to understand all you've been taught.

Does God speak to children? Yes, he does. He spoke directly to Samuel in his youth.

"And it came to pass at the time, when Eli was laid down in his place, and his eyes began to wax dim, that he could not see;
And ere the lamp of God went out in the temple of the Lord, where the ark of God was, and Samuel was laid down to sleep; That the Lord called Samuel: Here am I.
And he ran unto Eli, and said, Here am I; for thou calledest me. And he said, I called not; lie down again. And he went and lay down.
And the Lord called yet again, Samuel. And Samuel arose and went to Eli, and said, Here am I; for thou didst call me. And he answered, I called not, my son; lie down again.
Now Samuel did not yet know the Lord, neither was the word of the Lord yet revealed unto him.
And the Lord called Samuel again the third time. And he rose and went to
Eli, and said, Here am I; for thou didst call me. And Eli perceived that the Lord had called the child.
Therefore Eli said unto Samuel, Go lie down: and it shall be, if he call thee, that thou shalt say, Speak, Lord; for thy servant heareth. So Samuel went and lay down in his place.

And the Lord came, and stood, and called as at other times, Samuel, Samuel. Then Samuel answered, Speak; for thy servant heareth." I Samuel 3:2-10 (KJV)

    I believe He still speaks to children today. In previous chapters I have shared some of my experiences. There has been an open line of communication as we've walked out my life. Of course, much has changed. In the beginning I lacked knowledge, experience and spiritual wisdom. As a child, I had confessed my sins, invited Jesus into my life and accepted Him as my Lord and Savior, but it would take me years to fully understand Jesus's love and all He accomplished for me. I can still remember the atmosphere in the little white four wall church. There is no greater feeling than being in a room saturated by the Holy Spirit. I was surrounded by chaos, but I was unphased by it all. As I looked up towards the altar, I watched a heavenly glow fall and fill the room. A peace fell over me as I stood there. My spirit was drawn to the presence.

    The average person will just do what everyone else is doing or has always done. I've always been different in that way. As a child, I had lots of questions. I wanted to know why. *Why Jesus?* I must have asked God this question a million times in my youth. I just didn't understand why I needed to go through Jesus if I could communicate directly with Him. These are questions only a child would boldly ask our Almighty God. My heart was in the right place and I'm thankful for the special measure of grace I believe God has for children during their age of innocence. I do believe in the concept of the age of accountability. That children are not held accountable by God for their sins until they reach a certain age. And that if a child dies before reaching that age of accountability that child will by the grace of God be granted entrance into heaven. Everything God revealed to me in my youth set me up for future victories. The storms were on their way and the foundation laid during my age of innocence would give me a running start as a believer.

Jesus was a Jew, and the Jews are God's chosen people. Let us never forget this. We are grafted into the body of Christ through Jesus. We must accept Him as our Lord and Savior at salvation. Only His DNA and His blood can cover us. It permits us entrance into the kingdom of God and grants us access to all the benefits of His chosen people.

Jesus came down from His throne to experience what it was to be human. He became flesh which allowed Him an opportunity to understand the human experience. He is now able to relate to us. He understands what it is to be human and all the challenges that come with the flesh. He came down off His throne to become our relative. He is now able to not only understand this life, but He is able to speak and war on our behalf.

He was the perfect lamb and high priest all in one. The moment I truly grasped what this meant for me I broke down into tears and wept for a while. I was reading the book of Leviticus. There is much to be gained from the Old Testament. Especially, the "boring" books we'd rather just skip over. In my younger days, every year I would revisit the books in the beginning of the bible searching the scripture for deeper understanding, but nothing stuck out. For years, I read it and I got nothing out of it, but the literal meaning in the text. I just couldn't stop coming back to those books. I didn't know it at the time, but my spirit was being drawn to those books. God was answering my question. *"Why Jesus?"* It just took a few goes at it for me to see His answer. It had been right in front of me all along. I just couldn't see until God opened my eyes. He never changed how He was answering the question, but as I developed and matured spiritually those words began to come alive one day. The revelation hit me so strongly in my heart that all I could do was weep because in that moment I understood God's love for me.

    As you read Leviticus you see Israel encamped outside Mount Sinai while God appears in the Tent of Meeting dictating to Moses His specifications regarding the Jewish ceremonial laws. The laws are extremely detailed, outlining every aspect of how and when religious offerings are to be presented to God. God gives the instructions himself. At the ceremony God appears and engulfs the altar in a burst of flames. Soon after God also consumes two of Aaron's sons when they fail to make the right preparations for approaching the altar. And let us also keep in mind that even if there were no errors the sacrifice was only enough to atone for their sins a short time. Until Jesus. When Jesus was birthed into the earth, He became our kinsman. He was, is and will be the only man born without sin. He is the only man who will live without being tempted into sin. He was without speckle or blemish, but unlike the lamb he didn't atone for our sins. He paid the price to buy us back. We have been redeemed from the hands of the enemy. We'll never need to make another blood sacrifice after Jesus. He was also the perfect high priest. A man without sin able to stand between man and God and speak on our behalf. He literally is it all and accomplished it all for us. He provides a way for us to come to God without the fear of dropping dead in His presence because of our sins.

At the cross Jesus took our place. He bore our sin and died the death we deserved to die. He was our substitute. It was the ultimate example of love, and those who follow Him are expected to walk in that same kind of love. If we choose to follow Him, we must first lay down our life to walk with Him.

And finally, we must discuss relationship. Without a relationship with God all this means nothing. "*Why Jesus?*" You ask. Relationship. God has done all of this, so He could be in relationship with us. If I could only give one response to the question, *"Why Jesus?",* it would be this. God wants to be in an intimate relationship with us. I chose to discuss this last because I believe it is the most important take away from this chapter. If you only take away one thing from this book let it be this. God loves us. He loves us so much that He sacrificed His only begotten son, so we could have access to Him. He desires to walk and talk with us daily. He stands by waiting for us to grant Him access into our lives. He desires to teach us what He knows. He wants us to walk in spiritual truth and it is His desire that we reach our full potential. His desire is to bless us, but we must be in position for the blessing. Many Christians are focused on everything but the relationship with God. He created us for relationship. "*Why Jesus?* Jesus sacrificed His life to give us access to God. Jesus opened the door to it all. He is our way to the Father. I believe many don't have full understanding of the Holy Trinity. I've drawn that conclusion based on what I have witnessed. It appears to me that many Christians believe God and Jesus are one and the same, but they are not. Jesus is crucial in the life of believers, but it is important to remember that we walk out this life with the Holy Trinity backing us. God being at the top of that triangle. It is time that believers through Jesus begin to establish a relationship with God. I value God more than anything in my life. I love Him with all my heart. I'm so thankful Jesus died so I could have a relationship with God. I would have never made it this far without Him in my life. He continues to do a work in me and through me. Each season I grow to love Him even more and He never ceases to amaze me by the way only He can love me. Nothing compares to His unconditional love. Because of my relationship with Him I am now whole. His love alone fills me. Everything after that is a bonus. If you have been saved, but are struggling with your healing, deliverance and restoration; I'd encourage you to be honest with yourself as you evaluate where you are in your walk. Maybe you've experienced the Holy Spirit moving in your life. Maybe you've had an encounter with Jesus. But have you met God the Father?

Unshakable, Unbreakable

When I look at my life, I liken it to a quilt that God has been stitching together all along. Each season of my life a beautiful patch on its own that expresses His goodness, love and power. But as He continues to piece together the patches it is forming into an overwhelming expression of His glory. God being the master thread that holds it all together. A masterpiece that will hang in the Heavens and cause me to praise and worship Him eternally. Not only for all He has done, but for all that He is.

I have known God's voice since my early childhood. I have talked to Him. He has talked to me. I have trusted Him, and I believe He has come to trust me. From a young girl to a woman, we have walked out this journey together. Through my suffering He has held my hand. There hasn't been a moment He has left my side. He has wept with me and for me. When I fell He didn't just pick me up. He pulled on those things He placed inside of me, so I could pick up myself. He was there in every pit, and there were many. Always forgiving me of my human errors, reminding me of who I am, and showing me glimpses of what was to come. I had to only trust Him and continue to move forward. He was there in the darkness as all things around me ripped away at my essence. I was never alone. He was always there.

There were times I would wonder why He wouldn't stop my suffering. Why wouldn't He just relieve me of my pain? He could have easily changed my condition. Then I'd quickly be reminded in the spirit that He is God. The world is in His hands. All things are under His control. In those moments when I've lacked insight or understanding I've found peace in knowing that He is God. I don't have to know all the answers when He is with me.

I've learned to never think I have arrived with regards to wisdom. Only a foolish person would think they have reached the place of all knowledge and understanding. There is only one who is all knowing. That is God. There is a place we can arrive that is the pinnacle of all destinations. A place we are all ultimately striving toward when we begin our walk with God. That is to be with Him fellowshipping in His eternal glory. Since the beginning, everything He has done was so He could be in relationship with us. At the end of the day, everything means absolutely nothing if we don't have a relationship with God.

The Word has been key in my life. The Word is the key. It has unlocked doors giving God access into my life. It is spiritual food that continues to sustain me. It is a shifting agent that continues to bring about change in my life. The Word of God gives me life.

Faith is a seed. It is the seed that God has given us to grow our life into whatever it would be according to His will. And that's not even the best part of it all. What's so amazing is that no matter how big a life we could ever imagine for ourselves, it would still pale in comparison to what He has planned for us. His bounty is unimaginable. In the flesh we will never know the full magnificence of God. We can only taste and partially experience the magnitude of His power and love. What a mighty and wonderful God we serve.

It's unfortunate that some people are deceived into complacency, believing they have arrived. Those deceived become unteachable because in their minds they've surpassed all others in attaining the infinite wisdom that truly only God possesses. This is not to say they aren't knowledgeable, but we don't see the full picture. Reality spans so much further than we can grasp. God's vision line encompasses all things. I know my experiences are minimal compared to what He has and continues to witness take place across the earth. The spiritual truths I possess are only part of His infinite wisdom.

    In God's Word we have been advised to remain humble and warned about the consequences of pride. Don't let people make you feel more important than you really are. It's easier to remain humble when we keep Jesus as our standard. No one did this life better than him and no one ever will. I am constantly reminding myself no matter how much wisdom I acquire, it is still only a fraction of what is available. I don't allow my victories to lead me down a path of thinking I'm more spiritual or have more faith than others. I know that as life goes on, I will continue to hear the testimonies of others that will blow my mind. In comparison my life will seem like a walk in the park. I love to see others win. When one wins; we all win. Our victories are not about us. They aren't moments for us to shine, but opportunities for God to show us His glory.

    I know there are many today that doubt the existence of God. At least that's what they say. Some have been hurt, so they've turned away from God because life hasn't worked out the way they wanted. Others believe there is a God, but don't believe He still speaks. Well there is a God, and He still speaks. What others choose to believe does not affect what I know to be true. I can only imagine how hard it must be to understand something you've never experienced. It's often easy for us to dismiss things that don't line up with our reality. As believers we must refuse to allow the ignorance of others to deter us from the truth. Our walks are all very different. We are all unique creations with different assignments on our lives. It was intended for me to understand who I am. God revealed my purpose to me and showed me the vision for my life's call. I choose to move by His leading and His leading alone. In the end I will have to answer to Him.

    I turned forty-one this year and I feel as though I've already lived out a lifetime worth of experiences. Over time I have been able to have some amazing experiences, but on the flip side life wasn't always kind to me. I've been through and overcome so much. For years I fought to survive. I eventually ended up at a place where survival just wasn't enough. I was ready to live. I was alive, but I was not living. It was time for the chains to be broken so I could run free. I wanted to know joy and peace. What I desired most was love. Before I could receive the love I so desired, I would have to be delivered from the darkness within me, restored and made whole. That had been my journey thus far. God had spent all these years processing me out of brokenness to wholeness.

    I have always genuinely loved people. Some have made it very difficult to like them, but it has never stopped me from loving them. They may have given me every reason to shut them out of my life, and I have walked away from many relationships over the years because it was the easiest thing for me to do. Granted some relationships you need to flee from as fast as you can, but most often that is not the case. In the past, I didn't understand the beautiful part of dealing with the hard matters of a relationship and coming out on the other side together with a stronger bond. I didn't know because that hadn't been modeled for me.

I'm thankful to God for my personal processing. He did not set me up to fail. All the delays in my life have worked for my good. He slowed me down to show and teach me what it means and what it would take to be in committed relationships. He has made it plain and kept it real with me the entire way through. He has and continues to teach me in a way that I can relate and quickly gain understanding.

I'm relieved and excited that this part of my journey has come to an end. As I enter in the next chapter of my life, I begin to walk in divine purpose. Before we were born God had a great plan for our life. We were created for a purpose. We've been allowed to walk the face of this earth so we could be change makers. It is our responsibility to use our God given gifts, talents and abilities to make this world a better place. We will have to account for what we did and did not accomplish while we were here.

My life didn't start off too well. And that's okay. I understand now how the enemy used every opportunity he could when I was my most vulnerable to take me out. He knocked me down many times, but he couldn't keep me down. He knew what I carried inside of me before I had a clue. It has never been about me, but what God had placed inside of me. He did his best to take me out before I discovered my kingdom identity. If God be for me; who can be against me! I made it and I am completely intact! With God, I am UNBREAKABLE and UNSHAKABLE! I was built to war and win. And that's what I'm doing daily. I am winning for the Lord.

God has not wasted any opportunity as a teaching moment in my life. He has and continues to take me from faith to faith and from glory to glory. When I look back at some of the most difficult times of my life, I realize those are the moments he drew me closer to take me higher. God used those moments to launch me into something new. He transitioned me to the next level at those times. I had to see Him bigger and trust Him anew in those moments. What the enemy intended for my harm God used for my good. God is good and He doesn't drop anything bad into our lives. That goes against who He is. What He will do is take the bad in our lives and work it out for our good.

At this point in my relationship with God it has been proven that obedience is better than sacrifice. God has required me to do some radical things at times. I had to lose all concern for what others would think and follow through on what God had asked me to do. If we don't start and finish what we've been called to do, we will not walk in the fullness of what He intended for us. In this new stage of my life, I will not fight, but embrace the change.

While I was writing this book, I was attacked with negative thoughts. I began questioning myself. The fact that I was not a well-known public figure or an expert in a field caused some hesitation. It was challenging for me, but I had to push through that intimidation. Eventually, I was able to turn my mind away from those thoughts and move forward. It should never be a determining factor what we think we can or cannot do. We are nothing without God, but we can do all things through Christ Jesus if we believe.

It has always been a part of my destiny to write not only this book, but books. Before I was born it was written that I would write this book. I would have never thought I'd be sharing my story with the world, but here I am. And I now realize the importance of sharing our testimonies with one another. The more we share our life experiences with each other, the good and bad, the more we'll realize we have in common. Commonality allows us to relate to one another giving God an opportunity to bring us together.

What has happened to the love in Christianity? Isn't that the foundation of it all? God is love. All that He has done, including the sacrifice of his only begotten son, was because of His love for us. And we have been commanded to love others as He has and continues to show love for us. If we could just genuinely love one another the world would be a wonderful place. It's not impossible. This could be our reality. I can't control what others choose to do, but I choose to live a life of love.

It brings me great hope that God's chosen are beginning to manifest. Those who have been through the years of processing it takes to walk in maturity and be responsible with their anointing, spiritual gifts and assignments. What a day it will be when those that fellowship with God begin to show up making their mark on the church. Their faith and intentions have been tested, verified and approved. They have been anointed, appointed and released by God's authority. When they show up in the multitudes, the church will be restored. The church will regain its power and influence in society. It will function in authority. They will give God access to move on the earth mightily, establishing His kingdom as it was intended from the beginning.

As I conclude this book, I have a great sense of relief and peace. What a privilege it has been to tell His-story. Yes, His-story. It's my life, but His-story. I have survived to testify to the goodness of God. He has not let His word return void. What a journey it has been. It's a journey that ends in victory. I don't know who will read this book. I don't know whose life will be touched and possibly forever changed for the better due to His-story, but I know it's for someone. It's for someone so near and dear to God's heart that He compelled me to share my journey, so you could be encouraged.

Thank You

I could not end this book without acknowledging one special little girl. Thank you to Little Chundria. Where would I be without you? You are not forgotten. You were a smart, strong and brave little girl. Your survival instinct still amazes me. Your ability to compartmentalize trauma, repeatedly gather the little strength that remained, and continue to move forward is unbelievable. You had to grow up way too fast. I'm sorry for the years of innocence that were lost, but know they were not in vain. I stand here the woman I am today because of your sacrifice. I am living a life you could only imagine. I stand here today because you made a huge decision that would change the course of my life. You made a decision that would affect me for eternity. You answered "YES" to God when He called. What an enormous amount of faith that took for such a little girl. You are my she-ro. If I could travel back in time, I couldn't hug, kiss or thank you enough for what you have done for me. I will be forever grateful. There would be no me without you. As I move forward into the next phase of my life, I know that the time has come for me to let you go. We both knew that the road would eventually lead us here. As I sit here shedding tears of mourning mixed with tears of joy, I'm glad the day has come that you can finally rest in peace. Goodbye to you, Little Chundria. I will spend the rest of my days honoring you by living a life of which you would be proud.

To that Special Someone,

    If you are going through dark times and you feel alone. Believe me when I tell you; YOU ARE NOT! God is right there waiting to receive you. Just call on the name of JESUS and He will be there to guide you through. I have a very ugly past, but it didn't stop Him from loving me. He has gone over and beyond to win my heart and now I am sold out to Him. I can't help but be grateful for how blessed I've been through it all. Now, it is my reasonable service to be a blessing to others. Part of that blessing is the sharing of my testimony. Hopefully, it has shown you the awesomeness of the One and only true God. He is a God that will NEVER leave your side. He will guide you out of the darkness into the light. He will protect you and provide everything you need along the way. And if by chance you grow weary, so weary you lose the strength to even stand, you can rest in His hands. He will carry you. I love you! Don't give up! You will make it through! God bless you!

Chundria De'Antae

Notes